Good Graces

Invocations, Inspirations, Reflections
for Club Chaplains and Speakers

by

Patricia G. Warner, D.D.

Kate Bertin, Editor

First Edition
Othoreal Publishing Co.
Seal Beach, Calif.

Good Graces

Invocations, Inspirations, Reflections
for
Club Chaplains and Speakers
by
Patricia G. Warner, D.D.

Published by: Othoreal Publishing Co.
P.O. Box 2778
Seal Beach, CA 90740-1778

Copyright (c) 1993 by Patricia G. Warner
Kate Bertin, editor
Back cover Illustration by Bilko
Index by Index Plus
Printed by Ben-Wal Printing, Inc.
First Edition 1993, 2nd Printing 1993
Library of Congress Catalog Card #: 92-85276
ISBN: 1-882571-11-8

CONTENTS
Good Graces

Part I: IN THE BEGINNING

Chapter 1: The Sound of the Gavel 11

•Memo to the Presiding Officer

•The Chaplain of Choice

•Engaging Outside Clergy

Chapter 2: Kudos for the Club Chaplain 23

•You Are Important!

Chapter 3: Prayer Protocol 27

•Summary of Supreme Court Ruling on Prayers

•Why Pray?

Chapter 4: Devotional Types Defined 41

•Affirmations, Benedictions, Grace

•Inspirations, Invocations

• Meditations and Prayers

Chapter 5: Preparation 49

•How to Compose Your Own Good Graces

Chapter 6: Look to the Delivery 61

•Present Good Graces in Apropos Style

Part II: PRAYERS FOR ALL SEASONS

Chapter 7: Open the Meeting With... 69

 •Introductions into the Invocation 71

 •Short Invocations 77

 •Invocations with Scriptures or Quotations............81

 •General Invocations 89

 •Inspirations (Poems/Prose) 105

 •Special Prayers by Notables 127

Chapter 8: Good Graces 133

 •Table Blessings 135

Chapter 9: Benedictions 143

 •Close the Meeting with Blessings 145

Chapter 10: Special Events 157

 •Conventions and the Club Chaplain 159

 •Holidays and Patriotic Observances 171

 •Nationally Recognized Birthdays and Commem-

  orative Days 192

 •Invocations for Specialized Groups 209

Chapter 11: Memorial Services 219

 •Prayers and Inspirations for Organizations and

  Private Ceremonies

Part III: A TREASURY OF REFERENCE MATERIAL

Chapter 12: Bible Texts 243

>•Excerpts of favorite verses arranged in topical order

Chapter 13: Maxims into Life and Humor 273

>•Closing Thoughts for Newsletters, Church Bulletins, Speakers and Writers

Chapter 14: Gems of Wisdom 287

>•Ancient and Present Ideas to Capture Immortality

Appendix..303

>•**Resources: Where to Find It**........................305

Index 309

ACKNOWLEDGEMENTS

Goethe said there would be little left of him if he were to discard what he owed to others.

My primary "thanks" is to God for pragmatically directing my path to the persons who were to become my rooting section for inspiration, and to the gurus in the publishing field who so willingly shared their expertise.

Their combined efforts helped to make this book a reality, and they fulfilled the vision of the sage, who said, "There is no limit to what men can do, if they care not who gets the credit."

Without the Midas touch of Kate Bertin, the contents would still be in manuscript form.

My dear friend, Jean Sisco, was the "Pearl of Great Price" by providing inestimable contributions of acts, ideas, applause, faith and frank critique.

Press "Sister" Willodean Vance was my beacon of light, a guardian steering me from uncharted waters onto shallow ground.

And my beloved sisters, Jackie Day and Joline Fox, who, besides infinite support, aided in immeasurable ways.

I extend a bundle of love and hugs to my precious family, who cheered me on and gracefully relinquished their share of my time so that I could pursue this writing adventure.

Another giant debt of gratitude is due the following people who offered their knowledge and helped make this project possible: Earl Chessher, Jerry Cooper, Marilyn Merrill, Dan Poynter, Zia Rinker and Caroline Staff.

My heart is so thankful for these jewels in my life, and to the many friends and club colleagues who shared in this experience.

Whee — we all did it! Thank you, God.

—*PGW*

FROM THE AUTHOR:

THE TRIUMPH OF BOOKS

"When I consider what some books have done for the world, and what they are doing, how they keep up our hopes, awaken new courage and faith, soothe pain, give an ideal life to those whose hours are cold and hard, bind together distant ages and foreign lands, create new worlds of beauty, bring down Truth from heaven; I give eternal blessings for this gift, and thank God for books."

—James Freeman Clarke

Since recorded time, man has feebly attempted to put into words the whispers of infinite knowledge and the faint glimpses of eternity that God's grace bestows upon those with an unwavering faith in the divine, a receptive hearts and a soul seeking communion. The written word contains the key to the mysteries of life And without books, this book would not be possible.

Books are a treasure-house of the thinkers of the past, the gold-mine for the present and the bank for those mental giants to be born in the future. Books are priceless; they can inform, inspire and enlighten even the casual reader.

I thank God for the books in my library, which provide great pleasure and an invaluable service. Over a period of years, from these jewels, I have drawn upon so many resources that it is impossible to enumerate them.

All credits for the quotations, poems, sentiments and prayers are acknowledged when known. Any omissions of credits, upon notification, will be corrected in subsequent issues.

A special "thanks" to the known authors who added depth to this book by giving me permission to use their works, and also to the unknown authors who contributed their measure of material to this endeavor.

The genre of religious thought covered is broad in scope and hopefully universal in appeal, transcending theological divisions. Any form of prayer is in reality love in action, which knows no limitation of time and space and can be practiced in sweet silence or with group energies.

As "Good Graces" cannot possibly cover all the prayer facets required by the diversified types of organizations, resources have been included in the appendix.

It certainly is not a complete bibliography, as that would take volumes. Please use this sampling as a starter and as you "knock on the door" for guidance, you will magically and magnetically discover more material and sources of inspiration. Be receptive to your inner wisdom and take personal pleasure and pride in adding your gem of creative sparkle to your assignment or project.

I pray that those who read and savor this book will find many passages that will add enrichment to their daily living in countless ways.

God bless.

—*Pat*

PART I
In the Beginning

Chapter 1: The Sound of the Gavel
Chapter 2: Kudos for the Club Chaplain
Chapter 3: Prayer Protocol
Chapter 4: Devotional Types Defined
Chapter 5: Preparation
Chapter 6: Look to the Delivery

CHAPTER 1
The Sound of the Gavel

- Memo to the Presiding Officer
- The Chaplain of Choice
- Engaging Outside Clergy

A COLLECT

God bless our meeting here, dear Lord,
And all who share a part.
Guide us in the things we do —
Please, give us strength of heart.

We pray, may peace enfold our world
And we feel it from within
Standing proudly for the right,
But strong enough to bend.

We'll not forget to thank you, Lord,
For gifts from up above —
For country, friends and family,
For all the things we love.

And for all our other blessings
Too numerous to list,
For making our lives meaningful,
Not merely to exist.

—Pat Warner

CHAPTER 1

The Sound of the Gavel

MEMO TO THE PRESIDING OFFICER

The president of the women's club rose, tapped the gavel on the lectern and said, "Will the meeting please come to order... and in the absence of our chaplain, Mary Jane will deliver the invocation. Please rise."

A startled Mary Jane struggled to her feet, gulped and barely audibly spoke a few short sentences, then uttered a shaky "Amen."

The busy president had neglected to notify Mary Jane of her fill-in assignment. Even though the delivery of the invocation is a short presentation, it does usually require advance preparation.

The opening ceremonies of a meeting (invocation and/or inspiration, followed by the Pledge of Allegiance to the flag) is an important part of the program and should be presented in a meaningful manner.

An invocation:

• Aids in stilling the audience's minds to help neutralize the web of daily worries.

• Creates a feeling of peace and balance.

• Invokes a sense of unity that binds the membership and promotes dedication to the principles and goals of the organization.

• Adds dignity and a reflective atmosphere to the meeting.

Naturally, you do not want this ritual to be so reverent it becomes somber. A church bulletin board displayed this statement: "If a sad countenance is a sign of piety, the humble mule is the most religious of all."

After the opening ceremonies, your enthusiastic welcome and introductions will set the tone and put the membership in a receptive mood.

As presiding officer, you have worked your way up the chairs to your present prominent position and know that "Murphy's Law" is always lurking around the next corner. Despite a person's vision, capability, sense of responsibility and check-lists, to quote Robert Burn's famous saying, "The best laid schemes o' mice and men gang aft a-gley."

In truth, a president needs the flexibility of a chameleon and the stick-to-itive-ness of a pit bull to perform their demanding role. When you have dedicated and able assistants, you are indeed blessed, and it lessens the load.

This book is designed to aid you and your chaplain or inspirational chairman in fulfilling the important opening ceremony of your meeting with "Good Graces."

THE CHAPLAIN OF CHOICE

When your bylaws require that the office of chaplain/inspiration be appointed by the president, you have the freedom of choosing the most qualified person for this position. Unless your organization is of one devotion, you need not consider the candidates purely on their church or temple attendance. Any dedicated member can perform the lay-chaplain office aptly. Even the most unlikely person may turn saintly when given this responsibility.

Some presidents have complained that this office is not easy to fill. Many resort to begging, wheedling and cajoling members into acceptance. Hopefully, this book will correct that situation. After you have selected your lay-chaplain, you will be relieved of any further obligations of the chair, except for special events, which are also covered in *Good Graces.*

If your organization's bylaws do not cover the chaplain position, as is the case with many groups who meet infrequently, this floating assignment is filled by a random selection from the members attending. In such instances, the presiding officer could prepare an appropriate message, written on a 3x5 card, to be read by a member who is asked to fill the chaplain position without prior notice. This will help avoid embarrassment to a member who doesn't want to refuse, but is unprepared to meet the occasion.

Although a lay-chaplain need not be religiously devout, it is important that they are in accord with the accepted tenets of the majority of the membership.

The presiding officer would not want the "crowd critic" for the chaplain's chair. People prone to faultfinding often put others on the defensive, and this lack of credibility can soil the image of the office and negate the positive benefits of prayer.

Good luck on your choice of a chaplain. Remember, the member who accepts this appointment desires to serve you and the organization during your term of office. If you have any innovative ideas on the presentation of an inspiration, discuss it with your chaplain. Nothing bogs down an association like that old cliché, "But that's how we've always done it."

A sage once said, *"We are not here to do what has already been done."*

Even with the best-laid plans, emergencies arise. If, without previous notice, the chaplain is absent from the meeting and you feel unprepared to deliver an extemporaneous invocation, you may elect to say, *"In the absence of our chaplain, let us bow our heads in a moment of silence to acknowledge the loving presence of our creator. (Silence) Amen."*

SPECIAL EVENTS: A Break Away from Business

Special events are the fun times in club life. These out-of-the-ordinary occasions require a different approach in handling devotionals than the general meetings.

At banquets or luncheons, when the meeting is held in a different location, usually a restaurant or hall, in which outside guests are invited as part of the program, you will have to consider where to place your chaplain if he or she is to be included in the proceedings. When not seated at the head table, they should be at a table close to the microphone or to one that is available to perform their part in the ceremony without causing an awkward pause while reaching their station to speak.

At these affairs, you may want to suggest to your chaplain to impress and emphasize the theme of this special meeting into their presentation.

Some groups eliminate the invocation and/or The Pledge of Allegiance from their strictly social affairs. As presiding officer, you have that option. However, at meetings where a meal is served, a short presentation of a grace message lends a spiritual uplift to the occasion.

You must also decide if you want the audience to sit or stand during the presentation. Should you plan to have the salute to the flag or a patriotic song sung in solo or by assembly, you naturally ask the attendees to stand for the address to deity.

At conventions or other large gatherings, a guest clergyman, rabbi or priest may be invited to present the invocation or grace message. Do not take for granted that because of their experience, rank or title, they know exactly how to conduct the ceremony.

Some preachers have been known to push their personal

doctrines and deliver a sermon to these out-of-town visitors. As presiding officer, you should be explicit as to the time they are allowed to speak, and impress before-hand the theme of the occasion.

Payment of an honorarium should be as unobtrusive as possible. Be sure to include a "Thank you" whether they deserve it or not.

At one rather large convention, the host city had engaged the services of a minister and had neglected to order a meal or a place at a table for him. Being aware of pitfalls can make an ounce of prevention worthwhile.

Another suggestion: double-check that all the equipment needed for the ceremony is in place beforehand — the flag positioned, etc.

At a prestigious gala awards banquet, the program chairman had instructed honorees to march dramatically on stage to a specific marching tune. After dinner, the producer learned in horror that there was no piano in the hall for the pianist to play the highly rehearsed music.

Good Graces is not a cure-all for Murphy's Law, but it may alleviate some stress to know that your club chaplain is well informed, and at the "Sound of the Gavel" he or she will be prepared to present a meaningful message to the membership.

RETAINING OUTSIDE CLERGY

At a national convention, the president, who lived in another state, requested that the convention coordinator of the host city arrange the services of a minister to deliver the invocation before the awards banquet.

The night of the gala affair arrived. The president had requested that caterers place the salads on the table prior to the time of the slated dinner. After the delegates were seated, the president rose from the head table and introduced the guest minister. He then asked the assembly to stand for the invocation.

The minister marched to the microphone and began his dialogue with God. Reverently, the membership bowed their heads as he proceeded. He went on and on, and the audience grew restless and tired of standing at attention. Many began peeking to see if perhaps he was under a hypnotic spell, or even levitating. But apparently he had seized the opportunity to preach a full sermon to out-of-town visitors.

When the waiters began bringing trays of hot food to serve the head table, the president tugged at his coat. He quickly concluded, allowing the members to sit down and eat.

Because the minister stayed for the dinner and the program that followed, the president was unable to make an apology for this unseemly behavior by the clergyman. As the festivities that night concluded the convention, the president returned home pondering whether to ignore the event or publish a "sorry" notice in the group's monthly newsletter.

This is an extreme case — but if a guest minister knows the time allotted to the dissertation, it decreases the likelihood of such a thing happening.

A CHECKLIST

At conventions or other large gatherings, organizations may engage the services of an outside clergyman. The person or committee handling this assignment might consider the following:

- Is honorarium expected? If so, have treasurer make out a check beforehand.
- The proper title and correct pronunciation of his or her name
- Seating arrangement
- Validation of parking ticket
- Gratis meal ticket
- Assignment of member to greet and seat the guest
- Microphone, piano or other props needed
- With a tight schedule, will he or she stay the entire meeting? If not, arrange for an unobtrusive exit.

The guest should be informed of the following:
- When he or she is expected to speak
- The type of inspiratonal discourse desired (invocation; meditation; prayer; sermon; grace; etc.)
- Time allotted for speaking
- The purpose or intent of the meeting
- The theme of the meeting or motto of the organization
- Dress code — formal or informal

I offer my apology for bending to the urge to include the following poem, "Madam President," in this chapter, as I have no comparable piece of prose for male presidents.

Should someone submit a comparable poem in this vein, it will be included in the next printing.

—PGW

MADAM PRESIDENT
Unread papers on the floor,
Fingerprints affront the door!
No time to housekeep any more
    Since she's the President!

Unpressed linen on the chair,
Dust is dancing everywhere,
And cooking is a sad affair,
    Now that she's the President!

Members on the telephone,
Not a minute to call her own,
Sometimes she's weary to the bone!
    Busy, busy President!

Now to set her notes up straight
Can't afford to hesitate
And cause the meeting to run late,
    While she's the President!

Now, holy gee, how will she dress?
(This thing was worn ten times, I guess)
She swears they'll think her just a mess,
    And she is the President!

Grab a bite and hop a car —
Why does she have to live so far?
Hope this meeting's up to par!
    Worry, worry President!

The smile is brave, the spirit meek,
She taps the bell and starts to speak,
The voice is strong, but the knees are weak!
    Poor, poor President!

But suddenly, the flags appear —
And officers answer the roll call, "Here!"
Now duty prompts her, crystal clear —
    She is their President!

When all the chairmen have revealed
They've done their best in every field,
They stand for prayer, but her soul has kneeled —
    Grateful, happy President.

O, Freedom Land, how sweet your air!
Her God, her Flag, is all one prayer,
If she should weep she wouldn't care!
    For she's their Madam President!
                    —Thanks to an unknown author

CHAPTER 2

Kudos for the Club Chaplain

CHAPTER 2
Kudos to the Club Chaplain

Chaplain: A clergyman, or sometimes a layman, appointed to perform religious functions in a public institution, club, etc. (Webster's New World Dictionary)

YOU ARE IMPORTANT!

Cheers and congratulations to the Club Chaplain!

It doesn't matter whether you have been elected, appointed or volunteered for this office in your organization; you will gain in stature, self-esteem and spiritual awareness.

Rather than look on the chaplainship as a duty, consider it a glorious opportunity to serve. Your words can be a gift to the membership. One never knows what soul is plodding through the lonely wilderness of the mind, and a word or sentence may ease an aching heart and renew faith in the Infinite.

Prayer raises the level of consciousness of the membership. This awareness helps free mental tension and increase the flow of ideas and communication. The unity that your message can foster in the overall program is invaluable to any club. Invoking spiritual guidance for a meeting elevates it to a higher plane.

The preparation of your assignment — research, reading, writing and thought — will be mentally stimulating and help lend an air of peacefulness to your life. The type, style and technique of prayer can be as varied as your imagination permits.

Clubs are formed to accomplish certain objectives. Any time new ideas and free thoughts come forth in a group, there is progress.

Bertrand Russell once said, *"The demand for orthodoxy is stifling to any free exercise of intellect."* If you have some different ideas on ways to perform the chaplain's duties, other than what has been done in the past, talk to your president about it.

The purpose of this book is to give you "guide-lights" to aid in the planning, delivery and execution of all pertinent duties of the Club Chaplain. With protocol in place, you are at liberty to swell up your enthusiasm, prime up your poise and become Chaplain, magna cum laude.

"It is within my power either to serve God, or not to serve Him. Serving Him, I add my own good and the good of the whole world. Not serving Him, I forfeit my own good and deprive the world of that good which was in my power to create.

—*Leo Tolstoy*

•••

"Use what talents you posess: the woods would be very silent if no birds sang except those that sing best."

•••

CHAPTER 3
Prayer Protocol

- Summary of Supreme Court Ruling on Prayers
- Why Pray?

"Almighty God:

We make our earnest prayer that Thou will keep the Unit
States in Thy holy protection; that Thou wilt incline the hearts
the citizens to cultivate a spirit of subordination and obedience
government; and entertain a brotherly affection and love for or
another and for their fellow citizens of the United States at larg

And finally that Thou wilt most graciously be pleased
dispose us all to do justice, to love mercy, and to demean ourselv
with that charity, humility, and pacific temper of mind which we
the characteristics of the Divine Author of our blessed religion, ar
without a humble imitation of whose example in these things w
can never hope to be a happy nation. Grant our supplication, w
beseech Thee, through Jesus Christ our Lord. Amen.

—George Washingtc

CHAPTER 3
Prayer Protocol

When Gen. George C. Marshall received the Nobel Peace Prize is in 1953, he said, *"The most important thing for the world today is a spiritual regeneration that would establish a feeling of good faith among men generally."*

SUMMARY of SUPREME COURT RULING ON PRAYERS

Due to the Supreme Court ruling on prayers in public schools, many organizations have become skittish regarding the practice of having devotionals said at their meetings.

This need not be a delicate situation. To help dispel that cloud of doubt, the Supreme Court ruling summary is included in this chapter.

Presiding officers should keep in mind these facts:

•The Congress of the United States, both Senate and House, open their meetings with an invocation to God.

•Our courts use the Bible for oaths to validate statements of truth.

•"One nation under God" was added to the Pledge of Allegiance, which is in essence a prayer.

•The next-to-last verse of the national anthem, "The Star-Spangled Banner," reiterates this vow: "And this be our motto — 'In God is our trust!'"

•The famous statesman and third President Thomas Jefferson, author of the Declaration of Independence, wrote in the last sentence, "... with a firm reliance on the protection of Divine Providence."

•Even our money symbolizes our spiritual heritage. Every American coin or bill carries the motto "In God We Trust."

The basic precepts of our country are dedicated to a belief in God. Our rich religious inheritance should not be ignored.

The tradition of petitioning God for divine guidance at meetings is not only a spiritual act, but a patriotic one as well.

Benjamin Franklin asked for divine guidance when, during the framing of the Constitution, the state delegates at the assembly led by George Washington were, after four or five weeks of wrangling, no closer to unanimity than when they convened.

Franklin, addressing the chairman, said:

"In this situation of this assembly, groping as it were in the dark for political truth, and scarce able to distinguish it when presented us, how has it happened, sir, that we have not hitherto once thought of humbly applying to the Father of Lights to illumine our understanding?...

"Have we now forgotten that powerful friend? Or do we imagine that we no longer need His assistance?

"I have lived, sir, a long time (he was 82), and the longer I live, the more convincing proofs I see of this truth — that God governs in the affairs of men. And if a sparrow cannot fall to the ground without His notice, is it probable that an empire may rise without His aid?...

"I, therefore, beg leave to move that, henceforth, prayers imploring the assistance of Heaven, and its blessings on our deliberations, be held in this assembly every morning we proceed to business...."

This became the policy of the framers of the Constitution. The office of Chaplain of the United States was created in 1788 as an elected office and is still in existence.

The First Amendment to the Constitution declares that

"Congress shall make no law respecting an establishment of religion or prohibiting the free exercise thereof." But the document also clearly delineates a separation between church and state, a distinction that has caused controversy up to the highest court in the land.

The 30-page Congressional Research Report Service for Congress, revised Dec. 23, 1988, on "Prayer and Religion in the Public Schools: What is, and is Not, Permitted" summarizes the Supreme Court ruling as follows:

"'Government in our democracy, state and national, must be neutral in matters of religious theory, doctrine and practice. It may not be hostile to any religion or to the advocacy of no religion; and it may not aid, foster or promote one religion or religious theory against another or even against the militant opposite. The First Amendment mandates governmental neutrality between religion and religion and between religion and nonreligion.'" (Epperson v. Arkansas, supra, at 103-104)

Our basic American culture is represented by the Bible as the Judeo-Christian tradition.

Dr. Max Rafferty, former California State Superintendent of Public Schools, expressed concern over the Supreme Court ruling regarding prayer in public schools.

"I don't care whether a child is destined to be a Jew, Catholic, Protestant, Black Muslim, Holy Roller or ranting atheist. If he's ever to advance the slightest claim to being an educated man, he simply has to be intimately familiar with these and hundreds of other sublime stories which are the legendary landmarks of our whole Western civilization....

"And I'm not talking about religious treasures. I'm talking about cultural treasures."

It's no wonder that no other book can compete with the Bible for longevity or readership appeal. The 66 separate

31

books, written by more than 30 people over a period of 1,500 years, would be impossible to surpass, even in today's instant communication and computer technology.

If we had been born into another faith, our allegiance to the doctrines of our ancestry might well be what we would practice today. And for that reason, tolerance for all religious cultures needs to be established throughout the world.

In appreciation of the diverse doctrines in our country, the author has attempted to keep this book nonsectarian in scope, inviting the reader to select material that would not be contrary to the belief of the organization and to freely insert their creed into the message.

Most of these prayers and invocations are designed to cover nondenominational meetings. For a sectarian group, use a format that applies to the group's tenets.

WHAT'S IN A NAME?

Many non-sectarian clubs do not wish to be identified with a particular secular preference, and expressions contrary to a universal belief would not be appropriate. Some prayers do not mention the name of God but still recognize the Supreme Creator.

One very progressive chaplain handled the ethnic problem well by saying to her audience, "Let us each pray to the God we believe in."

In the spiritual literature of the world, the varying concepts of God are indicated by the use of such words as "Lord," "Father," "Mother," "Soul," "Spirit," "Principle," "Love," "Omniscient," "Life," "Infinite Intelligence" and "Creator."

People in the Western world generally use terms of reverence originating in the Bible; eg. Lord, Father, Almighty God,

Holy Spirit.

It is interesting to note that the name of God throughout the ancient and modern world mainly has four letters.

Lord — English	Soru — Persian
Deus — Latin	Gved — Flemish
Dieu — French	Deus — Portuguese
Gott — German	Adad — Syrian
Tixo — Zulu	Dodt — Dutch
Lian — Peruvian	Dodh — Danish
Baal — Phoenician	Dios — Spanish
Elah — Aramaic	Bram — Aryan
Jhvh — Hebrew	Teos — Greek
Buch — Slavic	Thor — Viking
Amon — Egyptian	Papa — Inca

(Notable exceptions are "Dio," Italian; "Bog," Russian; and "Allah," Arabic.)

Although the name of God is said in many different ways and languages, you need not be intimidated by using the words "Dear God" to address the Deity. All synonyms used to define God in any language are only the feeble attempts of our finite mind to describe the Infinite Source of all creation.

ONE BUT MANY

In a comparatively short period of time, the ethnic face of our nation has changed dramatically.

The diversity of cultures of our citizens has caused some universities to revamp curricula requiring undergraduate students to take courses in multicultural studies to better communicate in the workplace and on a social level. Exploring the history and culture of U.S. minority groups and foreign nations and those who speak a foreign language will be necessary for young people today to be effective in tomorrow's world. A global view with appreciation of each others' religion must be attained to ever realize our earnest desire for world peace.

Our visionary founding fathers gave us another motto to cover diversities in cultures: "E. Pluribus Unum" — "One but Many."

The heart of our nation and its people pulses in the security of prayer each time we pay for any kind of service — "In God We Trust."

A chaplain of a mixed denominational association is like the President of the United States and must represent all the people.

Because scripture verses from the New Testament would be unfamiliar and therefore less meaningful to people of the Jewish faith, the invocations that include these verses may not be appropriate for a meeting of mixed faiths. You will find an ample number of samples to meet that need.

When a chaplain can use Bible verses in the content of their prayer, the quotation often lends authority to the message. Because the Bible is a treasure chest of wisdom, it makes it an unlimited source for variety.

Many Christian and Catholic services end their prayers with the closing "through Jesus Christ our Lord. Amen." If members of the meeting are not all of the Christian faith, this conclusion may not be considered appropriate. A strong "Amen" would gracefully cover that situation.

Our constitution clearly guarantees that Americans of any religious persuasion can be accepted into the whole of society. This touch with other faiths does not inhibit our awareness, but expands it. We are blessed with beliefs of every religious denomination: Christianity, Confucionism, Hinduism, Judaism, Mohammedanism, Metaphysics, Protestantism, Zoroastrianism and others — all separate creeds, each worshipping One God in their own way.

When we as individuals and as a nation come clearly to the truth, that we are all part of the human family and are living on one planet in the ever-evolving universe with no "exit" signs around, we may consider "Universal Brotherhood" a comfort. And, perhaps, heed the wisdom of George Washington when he said, "*Observe good faith and justice toward all nations. Cultivate peace and harmony with all.*" Races and religions must find a cohesiveness, a harmony.

The riots in the 1960s did not solve the problem, and the 1992 riots that fractured Los Angeles, leaving the city in flames, clearly demonstrated the desperate need for multiculturalism. When we as individuals, as groups, as communities, as cities, as states, as a country, can free our minds of separateness and think in terms of brotherhood of all mankind, we will be blessed and know the joy of freedom from fear.

Respecting one another's doctrines is not only charitable, it is a requisite for being a virtuous person with a permit to be part of the human race.

Bigotry in any form is not compatible with holiness. We all worship one God; it matters little what path to the Kingdom we tread. Service, love and reverence for life is the only payment we can give our Creator for the gift of life.

How many of us today want to go back to just a "living on the land" style of existence? We do not raise bananas or coffee, we do not want to spin and weave our garments; we are in a true sense interdependent on the toil and talents of others throughout the world. When that dependency turns to gratitude, then we will practice the admonition of the Scriptures,

"Love thy brother as thyself." We will reap the tangible blessing of the three Cs: Communication, Cooperation and Consideration.

Differences in creeds make no difference at the Veteran's Hospital in Long Beach, Calif. There is a warm and inviting chapel on the second floor where Jewish and Protestant services are held each week and on special religious and patriotic holidays.

Chaplain Rev. George Vogel pointed out two wooden hand-carved symbols about two feet high on the altar. One was a Jewish Star of David; the other, a Christian cross, made by the same craftsman. Each is displayed according to the service being held.

The Rev. Vogel, Rabbi Sidney Guthman and the other chaplains assigned to the hospital devote their time and energies to each patients' needs regardless of their religious affiliation.

When the 1989 earthquake struck in Fullerton, Calif., the charming old vine-covered brick church owned by the Church of Religious Science was severely damaged.

Months went by before it was determined whether it could be restored or rebuilt. In the interim, the Jewish Temple generously offered its facilities so that the Sunday services could be resumed.

These incidents and thousands of others throughout this land prove that Americans are living the motto handed down by our forefathers — "E. Pluribus Unum" — "Many but One."

"God grant that not only the love of liberty, but a thorough knowledge of the right of man, may pervade all nations of the earth so that a philosopher may set his foot anywhere on its surface and say, "This is my country."

—Benjamin Franklin

WHY PRAY?

A recent bumper sticker read, "Prayers will never be outlawed in schools as long as teachers give tests."

Asking "Why do we pray?" is like asking, "Why do we breathe?" — it just seems so natural. Even people who do not practice any formal type of prayer pray unwittingly. Formless prayer without words can carry power; it is the deep intent, the idea and belief that determines the strength.

Scientists claim we think only one thought at a time, but are able to handle 200 thoughts a minute. Prayer tempers the racing mind, allowing ideas to focus in a more relaxed atmosphere, thereby transmuting power into thought.

History records the great souls of all ages have used prayers to help lift banners of victory against the powers of darkness.

● ● ●

"It is the duty of all nations to acknowledge the providence of Almighty God, to obey His will, to be grateful for His benefits, and humbly to implore His protection."

—George Washington

● ● ●

"Prayer is the time exposure of the soul to the highest that we know, and he who practices it will learn its central, primary and transforming importance. Prayer is the fulfillment of man's highest capacity to look not down alone nor out, but up, and to adore. Prayer is the road to the crowning experience of human life, being carried out of ourselves by something greater than ourselves to which we give ourselves. Prayer is taking in earnest the central affirmation of religion that there is a responsive Spirit at the heart of reality in communion with whom is our power and peace. True prayer is never an endeavor to change the divine purpose, but is always an endeavor to release it through the one who prays into the world."

—Harry Emerson Fosdick

• • •

"Our prayers should be for blessings in general, for God knows what is good for us."

—Socrates

• • •

"...man is confronted by something spiritually greater than himself which, in contrast to human nature and all other phenomena, is Absolute Reality. Man's goal is to seek communion with the Presence behind the phenomena, and to seek it with the aim of bringing his self into harmony with this Absolute Reality."

—Arnold J. Toynbee

• • •

"When thou prayest, rather let thy heart be without words than thy words be without heart."

—John Bunyan

• • •

"Every Christian needs a half an hour of prayer each day, except when he is busy, then he needs an hour."

—*St. Francis de Sales*

• • •

"Prayer is not an old woman's idle amusement. Properly understood and applied, it is the most potent instrument of action."

—*Mahatma Gandhi*

• • •

"You pray in your distress and in your need, would that you might pray also in the fullness of your joy and your days of abundance."

—*Kahlil Gibran*

• • •

"Prayer takes the mind out of the narrowness of self-interest, and enables us to see the world in the mirror of the holy."

—*Abraham Joshua Heschel*

• • •

"Certain thought are prayers. There are moments when, whatever be the attitude of the body, the soul is on its knees."

—*Victor Hugo*

• • •

"Pray inwardly, even if you do not enjoy it. It does good though you feel nothing, even if you think you are doing nothing."

—*Julian of Norwich*

• • •

"Pray as you can, for prayer doesn't consist of thinking a great deal, but of loving a great deal." —*St. Teresa of Avila*

• • •

As though the preceding quotations did not cover the question, "Why pray?," the author has taken the liberty to include her ponderings on this subject.

This chapter has been included, not to convince you of the benefits of prayer, but to help stimulate your thoughts regarding it when composing your own prayer messages for meetings or personal use.

• • •

The purpose of prayer is to nurture our celestial instinct, a cup held up to be filled with the elixir from the spirit of God to satisfy the longing in our heart and bring peace and understanding to the mysteries of life. Prayer helps us rise above the storms of human existence and salves the cryptic mind to allow us communion with our supernal Source. Prayer to man is like nectar to a bee and can still the inner longing for love as it touches our soul.

• • •

Prayer is an eager outpouring of our subtle soul seeking to touch the Eternal Source.

• • •

Prayer is the inner soul of man stretching toward the unknown Reality of God.

• • •

Prayer is man's eternal quest for contact with the all-prevailing Supernal Power of the universe and galaxies.

• • •

Prayer soothes the soul by filling a latent desire to make contact with the higher realms of Being.

• • •

Prayer is a form of surrender to man's innate need to correspond with the higher Realities of the supernal splendor of God's infinite Kingdom.

• • •

CHAPTER 4
Devotional Types Defined

- Affirmations, Benedictions,Graces
- Inspirations, Invocations
- Meditations and Prayers

CHAPTER 4
Devotional Types Defined

Affirmations

Many religious groups practice prayer in the form of affirmations. These may be recited in unison by the group or voiced by the leader.

Generally, affirmations vary from the formal type of prayer in that one is not requesting God's divine grace be bestowed on a particular subject. It is a statement of beliefs that one wants affirmed by a higher power, as expressed in the Scriptures, "I believe; help my unbelief!" (Mark 9:24)

Affirmations have been used quite effectively in reinforcing a positive thought pattern into the subconscious, or to help eliminate a negative, unworthy one. This practice has proved most beneficial by therapists in treating their clients.

As that ancient philosopher, Plotinus, said, "Thought and thing depend upon and correspond to each other."

Affirmations can add an added dimension to the depth of one's belief because they are making a statement of truth that they believe or want to believe is a truth. The wording in this type of devotional is often changed from "Please, God..." to "I am..." stated in a positive fashion.

Benedictions

A benediction is a short message requesting God to oversee the safe return home of the membership and their well-being while being absent from one another. Because of the brevity of this injunction, it is very difficult to add variety to the few sentences — a challenge to the ingenuity of a chaplain.

Closing Thoughts

Some clubs use this thought-provoking method of closing a meeting on an upbeat note. It need not have inspirational value, and it is often more appreciated if it is in a humorous vein.

A wise man once said, "... send them away laughing, and they will come back."

Refer to chapters 13 and 14 for a wide selection of closing thoughts to inject a bit of blessing, humor or inspiration into the meeting.

Examples and samples of all forms of prayer discourses are in Part II of this book.

Peruse and use those that seem suitable. But don't discount the personal satisfaction to be gained by creating your own original messages of inspiration. You will find it a rewarding experience that adds a new dimension to your life.

Grace (or Table Blessing)

Grace is a message to the Infinite expressing gratitude for material blessings and may be delivered before or after the meal. It is related mainly to food and thanksgiving, although the purpose of the meeting may be mentioned briefly. The most common custom is to say grace prior to the meal; however, in instances where some tables have been served and the guests are eating, it may be very awkward to interrupt the service. In this case, grace may be said after the meal. This delivery should be reverent and very short. The membership may sit or stand during this presentation.

Inspiration

The inspirational message is in a lighter focus. A reflective poem, prose, quotation or reading from great works of literature that has an uplifting effect on the emotional senses could be considered an inspirational discourse. It may be read, and the author should be given credit if the author is known.

This kind of presentation need not be delegated only to one person. The presiding officer in the organization may wish to rotate this pleasurable task. Although it is not a dialogue with the deity, the content should be of a quality that lifts one's spirits or has a profound statement worthy of consideration for greater insight, which would benefit all those in attendance.

The inspiration may be inserted into the meeting agenda any time that seems appropriate. Sometimes the Pledge of Allegiance will precede this presentation. Because there is no restriction on the length, the membership need not stand.

Invocation

An invocation for a meeting often is a request to a higher power for divine guidance. It should be so stated to fit the particular needs of the membership. Generally, it is presented as an opening exercise. However, it also is proper to use at the close of a meeting.

The length of the invocation may vary, but most assemblies prefer it to be a short dissertation, no longer than one or two minutes.

As a rule, the invocation precedes the Pledge of Allegiance (God before country). The audience stands for this presentation.

•••

"For where two or three are gathered together in my name, there am I in the midst of them." (Matthew 18:20)

•••

Meditation

A meditation is a discourse in a different vein than a prayer, in that the person who is mediating normally does not beseech the deity to bestow infinite blessings, but rather seeks to still the mind to reach a contemplative state to be receptive to the higher planes of thought — an act of intent to listen for whispers of the inner intuitive voice, or to reach that elusive place of reverie of which the poets speak.

Study groups and religious gatherings often use this form of communion. There is no set time frame to hold a meditation, as each assembly determines its preference; at the beginning, middle or close of the meeting. It can be a guided session where the leader takes the participant through mind visualization to a scene of serenity. Meditations are usually based on religious or philosophical subject matter, and most generally carry one central theme or thought. A period of silence may follow the meditation presentation, to allow the Divine Power to commune with the soul of the listeners.

Prayer

A prayer is very similar to the invocation, an entreaty or supplication to God. It differs, for unlike the invocation used mainly to open or close a meeting, a prayer may be said at any time during the meeting. Sometimes there is a set formula, such as the Lord's Prayer, that is recited by the assembly, or a religious poem or the dedication to the creed of the organization, delivered in unison or by the group leader. Experienced speakers and the clergy have practiced the art of spontaneous prayers to perfection, which may be difficult for the laity.

Prayers, like invocations, may include Bible verses or works of authors in the content.

The audience may be seated or stand during this presentation.

•••

The many definitions of "Prayer" are so general that any of the devotionals defined could also be considered a form of prayer.

The author has taken this means of clarifying the terminology used in this book. Other interpretations or classifications of inspirational discourses for meetings practiced by any group would naturally be valid, as no set authority in this field has been certified.

Samples and examples of all forms are included in Part II.

CHAPTER 5
Preparation

• How to Compose Your Own Good Graces

CHAPTER 5

Preparation

HOW TO COMPOSE A MEANINGFUL MESSAGE

Author's note: This chapter is included for the lay-chaplain who may not have had previous experience in writing or preparing devotionals. Experienced chaplains and clergy may find this primer material and are invited to browse lightly or ignore solidly.

COMPOSING A HOMILY: IT'S EASIER THAN YOU THINK

Contrary to what you may think, composing your own invocations and grace messages is not that difficult.

To a novice, any task may seem formidable until the knack is known. The knack for creating your own prayer lies in the discipline of the mind, and that is a formidable task!

Calming racing thoughts can be like chasing butterflies in a windstorm. Prayer helps attune to higher realms of consciousness and proclaims supremacy over the busy, image-making mind, which is prone to dwell on the surface irritations instead of looking beyond the passing scene and changing elements of daily life.

Solitude and silence is needed by most people to obtain that state the ancients called "The secret place of the most high," a retreat or surrender of the inner soul stretching toward union with the Infinite Source. Prayer is recognition of God's ever-present grace flowing to meet all needs. In these moments, flecks of inspiration can dance through the mind like fireflies at twilight. When your intuitive antenna is up, it would be well to have a pad and pencil on hand to jot down these fleeting ideas, which will aid you in producing prayers of substance.

With today's bustling schedules, planning times of silence can be a problem. Sometimes stepping inside a local church may lend an air of peace to your mind and body. The reverent atmosphere allows you to stand back in detachment and look at the overall weaving pattern, not just the knots and tangles of life.

Even a short visit to the park may help. Watching a sunset can stir a feeling of awe that will inspire your innate creativity.

Try awakening before the hustle of morning activities to capture some moments of serenity and solitude.

After you have found a place of quietness and a sense of reverie, sometimes repeating great, familiar words will help you sustain that mood — for instance, "love," "peace," "God." Some people use excerpts from favorite Bible quotations. "Be still and know... God." "The earth is the Lord's, and the fullness thereof," "I will never leave Thee or forsake Thee," "Lo, I am with you always," "This is my beloved child, in whom I am well pleased," "Not my will...Thy will be done."

Reading an inspirational poem or saying an affirmation also is helpful in coaxing the mind to surrender to a more peaceful atmosphere and aids in releasing body tension. We have been told that mental tension and body tension walk hand in hand. The ability to clear discordant thoughts from your mind and retreat from dull routine realities is an act that will lift your spirits and add a deeper enjoyment to life.

"And thine ears shall hear a word behind thee, saying, This is the way, walk ye in it, when ye turn to the right hand, and when ye turn to the left." (Isaiah 30:21)

Here is a short affirmation you may want to try:

"Today, I prepare myself to be open and receptive to God's guidance. All fear and frustration disappear from my life. I am secure in the loving, protecting Spirit of God. I recognize the Divine Urge within to express, and in perfect confidence I leave my affairs in the hands of this Principle. I cooperate with it.

"I take one step at a time, not feeling rushed or hurried, for God's universal plan of right action is infinitely designed, sustained and marketed in divine order.

"I give thanks, Dear God, that today I am privileged to be the instrument through which Thy holy inspiration flows."

●●●

I AM OPEN AND RECEPTIVE TO THE CREATIVE POWER WITHIN

Dear God,

I thank you for this beautiful day. It is a special day in which I expect to accomplish all that I set out to do. Please direct my thoughts and actions on the path that will give the greatest impulse to my creative urges.

May I keep so attuned that this inspiration will allow me the follow-through for all my efforts. Almost is not enough. I pray my mind becomes a channel of direct action and decisiveness.

Keep my heart and spirit glad that I am able to pursue my self-appointed goals. When I know that what I am doing is right, I can rest in the knowledge that back of every idea is its perfect fulfillment. Let me envision only the completed task. Consciously, I now eliminate all doubt barriers from my mind. Only a mushroom reaches maturity overnight. Grant me the patience to allow my idea-plant to blossom and ripen in due season.

I ask that my accomplishments serve and benefit my

fellowman. Let me sow seeds for the strength, courage and wisdom to carry me to the conclusion of a rewarding harvest.

"Do not be deceived; God is not mocked, for whatever a man sows, that he will also reap." (Galatians 6:7)

After you have conditioned your mind and uplifted your attitude, thus allowing the seed ideas planting space, you are ready to put the five ingredients to success to work.

Our mind is a powerful instrument that can be used to create chaos or peaceful dominion. We have the choice. Be not cautious — dare to use the magic formula: mind power, the key to the kingdom, to unlock the genie of life.

1. Imagination — starts thinking
2. Visualization — starts belief
3. Belief — starts the flow of creative forces
4. Faith — adds fuel to fan the flames of success
5. Action — brings the invisible into manifestation

WHAT TO WRITE

When composing your own prayer, try to focus on one theme, as only a short message is allowed. You will want to make a potent statement that will strike a chord in the heart of your audience.

What is every person's true desire? Peace would be one of the items at the top of the list. Freedom, also, would rate very high: freedom from pain, freedom from financial burdens, freedom from worry and frustration, freedom from false appetites and pessimistic habits and thoughts.

Buoyed-up self esteem also will help one reach that peaceful retreat like a pool in the rapids. Each person is like an iceberg, seven-tenths under water. That inner depth that is not visible on the surface holds the divine spark. By words, you can kindle a flame to light up the darkness of the inner soul.

Encouraging, inspiring words can conquer despair.

Place self esteem high on the list for the theme of your homily.

"Since we have the same spirit of faith as he had who wrote, 'I believed, and so I spoke,' we too believe, and so we speak." (II Corinthians 4:13)

Although a public prayer is only a few ticks on the clock of time, the utterance of appropriate words with meaning can strike the sensitive heart-chime of those who participate. You want your audience to enter into the solemn simplicity of opening a two-way channel between them and God; the purpose of all prayers. The recognition of the availability of the Divine Creator is in itself a prayer.

The words need not be loud, but earnest and sincere. The spoken word has power and is 80 percent stronger than a word read or thought.

Words create images in the mind. Words can also incite reactions of antagonism or love. The use of proper words to set the tone of your meeting will be reflected in the attitude of the assembly.

Ad copy-writers long ago discovered the potency of using power words in their advertising to influence the consumer. Subliminal advertising in television commercials has been under public censure. Music is a more subtle form of persuasion, perhaps more effective, as it strikes the chord to one's heart-strings and has a more lasting emotional effect on the hearer.

Singing even increases the strength value. The more senses that are brought into play, the greater the impact on our emotions. There are organizations that have songs members sing as a part of their service, either at the beginning or at the end of their meetings.

Because you are making a verbal delivery, you should take into account that the person hearing the words does not want to strain to hear or understand the words. Try to inject calming, comforting, uplifting words in short sentences that are easier to assimilate.

If your group has a set format for invocations, prayers or grace, be cautious in veering from the normal procedure. Many people are uncomfortable with a change of customs, and nobody wants unsettledness in the ranks over prayers.

An invocation at an association meeting may be a form of ritual, but it need not be a type of rote prayer. This public conversation with God should be on the same friendly level you would use when privately conversing with God. Talk to Him as naturally as you would your own earthly parent who deeply loves you. We need not be formal; God does not treat us as strangers.

All devotionals should be in a positive vein, without judgement or criticism. It is not appropriate to compose a prayer that puts a competing group down, asking the Infinite to help your cause over another one. It is proper in this instance to request guidance, strength and energy to unite your desire for victory. Asking a blessing for your team and a blessing for the adversary would add a benevolent tone to the message.

No matter how deeply involved you are in your own creed, it is improper to impose these beliefs on your captive audience. One president lost sleep over that delicate situation, in which she hesitated to censure the chaplain for doing this.

A point to remember: even experienced chaplains can forget that an invocation is not a mini-sermon. In fact, it usually is the professional speaker who delivers over-extended homilies.

Every association has its own philosophy, purpose, goals or image. Very often, the constitution and/or bylaws includes an article listing the objectives of the organization. Clubs of a less formal nature may have a motto or song or poem that aptly expresses the deep heart intent, the reason for their existence.

By careful study of these written creeds you, as chaplain, can incorporate the principles and ideals into the theme of your prayer or invocation.

Your willingness to be club chaplain and serve your organization and the membership will be a blessing for them and to yourself. Remember that gifts freely given to others are not altogether altruistic, for in giving, one also receives in many almost magical ways.

Although there are no "Robert's Rules" for public prayers, you may feel more comfortable having a formula for reference when creating your own original discourses. The following suggestions are intended to be only guidelines. However, the best guideline is the subtle dictates of your heart. When there is conflict between heart and head, we have been told to follow the heart action, as its motives are of a purer quality than our mental faculties.

Because of the limited time allotted for your presentation, you will not be able to incorporate all these ideas into your composition. Give preference to those which suit your needs and the audience you are addressing. The text should be flexible and have reference to the occasion.

FORMULA IDEAS FOR FRAMING AN INVOCATION

1. Introduction (Optional) — If needed to gain quiet or attention. Also may be used to preface and reinforce the message. (*Examples follow this outline.*)

2. Salutation — Dear God; Lord; Our Father; Almighty God; Our Creator and Sustainer of the Universe; Our Heavenly Father; Dear Holy Spirit; Father, Mother, God; Our beloved Lord of all; Great God and Father of us all; Eternal God; Dear Lord and Savior, Jesus Christ*

*Use only when the whole assembly is Christian.

3. Recognition
- Theme of the meeting — special occasion, etc.
- Relate to the purpose of the organization — Educate, fellowship, influence, inform, motivate, network, service. Quote a club motto, an appropriate axiom or related Scripture verse.

4. Gratitude — Acknowledgement of blessings.

5. Request wisdom and guidance for leaders in performance of duties.

6. Ask Divine assistance in achieving goals and aspirations.

7. Petition that blessings be bestowed upon the membership, parent organization and absent and ill members (optional).

8. Solicit for benefits to the members for their attendance.

—Pray that each take from the meeting a spark of inspiration, an idea or nugget of truth to make the donation of their time worthwhile.

9. Entreaty for God's loving care to be bestowed on any disaster situations at home or abroad. Include the hungry, helpless and needy people of the world.

10. Pray that divine guidance be steadfast in the hearts and minds of all world leaders.

Praying for, asking for and visualizing world peace is the greatest gift a group can give to our times, our children, our beautiful planet Earth and God. *"If two of you agree on earth a bout anything they ask, it will be done for them by my Father in heaven." (Matthew 18:19)*

11. Quote Bible verse here if appropriate (optional) Some organizations of mixed denominations prefer verses of scripture not be included in the invocation. When this is the case, the chaplain can adjust to this unwritten rule.

12. Conclusion: Amen.

The use of the expression "Amen" at the conclusion of a prayer is approprate for mixed denominational meetings, as the term is used in many languages.

The Hebrew word "amen" means true, faithful, certain. It also is used in the end of prayer as an earnest wish to be heard; amen, so be it, it shall be so.

A reminder: The length of the invocation or prayer is an important feature of your presentation. Due to that fact, you would have difficulty in incorporating each segment of this format into one message. This formula is a simple guideline to assist you when you wonder what points you wish to cover in your prayer service.

INTRODUCTIONS
"Shall we pray so our thirst will be satisfied?"
Dear Lord:

• • •

As a beautiful sunset can put a song of serenity in our hearts, so too can prayer create harmony and a spiritual bonding that adds beauty and joy to the issues of life. Let us pray.
Dear God:

• • •

As we come together to renew our dedication to the noble principles upon which this organization is founded (motto). We enter to learn, we go forth to serve. We pray that we may be fulfilled inwardly as we serve others outwardly.
Dear God:

• • •

As the future of mankind depends upon his moral nature, let us be in the vanguard as shining examples of that high estate.
Almighty God:

• • •

We know the secret of life is outpouring, not taking in, so by our association in this organization we are blessed with the opportunity to expand individually, mentally, morally and spiritually.
Let us give thanks. Dear Father:

• • •

A scripture verse may also be used as an introduction:
"For where two or three are gathered together in my name, there I am in the midst of them." (Matthew 18:20)
Let us pray, secure in the promise our prayers will be heard.

CHAPTER 6
Look to the Delivery

•Present Good Graces in Apropos Style

"Though I speak with the tongues of men and of angels, and have not charity, I am become as sounding brass, or a tinkling cymbal. And though I have the gift of prophecy, and understand all mysteries, and all knowledge; and though I have all faith, so that I could remove mountains, and have not charity, I am nothing. And though I bestow all my goods to feed the poor, and though I give my body to be burned, and have not charity, it profiteth me nothing."   *(I Corinthians 13:1,3, KJV)*

CHAPTER 6
Look to the Delivery

PRESENT GOOD GRACES IN APROPOS STYLE

The delivery of an invocation or inspirational message is not an impromptu act except, perhaps, for the very experienced speaker. Even people in the ecclesiastical community may need the security of a draft when saying prayers before an audience. Extemporaneous blessings are not easy.

There was a popular but small church in Orange County, Calif. that had an energetic minister who said the same prayer to the congregation each week. Finally, one of the parishioners asked, "Is that prayer our ritual or statement of our doctrine?"

Sheepishly, the pastor replied, "No, that happens to be the only one I have memorized, and I have a reading problem."

Some lay people are well qualified to give spontaneous invocations and are encouraged to do so. However, it is recommended that one's own religious preference is not made obvious in the presentation.

Many meaningful messages, well prepared and written down, have been lost to the membership because of poor delivery. Though you may "speak with the tongues of men and angels," if you don't have a listener with ears to hear, your efforts will not be rewarding.

If you write all the material down and practice reading it aloud for several days before the date of the meeting, preferably in front of a mirror, the message will be firmly inplanted in your mind. Many public speakers tape their talks and listen to it for proper inflections and vocal imperfections.

An address to the deity should be spoken at a slower rate than normal speeches or conversation. Speak distinctly so the membership will comprehend what it is you are saying. Decreasing the tempo of your talk will lessen any nervousness and help you from faltering over the pronunciation of unfamiliar words.

Find out from the presiding officer during which part of the meeting you will be called upon to speak. Knowing when you are scheduled on the program will keep anxiety at a minimum.

If the membership is to rise during your invocation or inspiration, the presiding chair should make the request by saying, "Will you please rise. The invocation (prayer) will be given by our club chaplain, John/Susie Jones."

If you are seated with the audience, rather than at the officer's table, you may wish to be standing close to the podium when the president calls the meeting to order, so you do not have the whole assembly watch you as you walk to the microphone.

Some men have booming voices and do not need the aid of an amplifier in a small room. Unless you can be distinctly heard by every person in the meeting room, you should use a microphone.

It is not necessary to address the chairperson or president. Always pause and wait until the noise of people's chairs scraping the floor subsides before proceeding with your presentation.

If, after waiting for quiet, there is still a state of unsettled-ness, command attention with an introductory remark. Use a Bible verse if appropriate: As Paul said, "Think on these things.'" Or, refer to the section titled "Introductions" in the chapter on invocations.

When you elect to read your discourse, have notes written or typed on a 3x5-inch card that can be held in the palm of your hand or placed on the lectern. You need not bow your head. Your voice should not be aimed at the floor. Practice speaking to the person in the last row of the audience.

Although the membership will usually instinctively bow their heads, any audience has "peekers," so your posture can be important.

Stand on both legs evenly. Leaning on one leg or the other will give an ungraceful appearance and detract from your message. Dangling or large jeweled earrings also are a distraction.

Speak in a clear, slow, reverent tone, but not softly.

Practice being confident and unhurried with this presentation. The more relaxed you are, the more sincere and spontaneous your message will sound.

Always end with a strong, distinct "Amen" so the membership will know when you have concluded your part in the program.

If the meeting is not of a religious nature and the membership is of mixed denominations, you may want to avoid the familiar Protestant ending, "In Jesus' name we pray." Refer to the chapter on prayer protocol for more discussion on this issue.

PART II:
Prayers for All Seasons

- Chapter 7: Open the Meeting With...

- Chapter 8: Serve Grace With Meals

- Chapter 9: Close the Meeting with Benedictions

- Chapter 10: Special Events

- Chapter 11: Memorials

CHAPTER 7
Open the Meeting with...

- •Introductions
- •Invocations
- •Inspirations (Poems and Prose)
- •Individualized Prayers

•Shall we bow our heads as we take this moment to commune with our Infinite Source. Our Father: ...

● ● ●

•Let us now pause to acknowledge the supreme Creator of our universe. Dear Lord: ...

● ● ●

•As we retreat from the tumult of daily living, let us be open and receptive to God's unfailing guidance. Dear God: ...

● ● ●

•As we step aside from the world of material sense and humbly acknowledge our many blessings, let us pray. Our supernal God: ...

● ● ●

•Let us now stand and request that God's government guide us in all our undertakings. Dear God: ...

● ● ●

•As we quiet ourselves to feel God's omnipresence, let our inner ear be open to the "still small voice" and our hearts be filled with universal love. Dear Lord:

● ● ●

•Let us take this moment in loving awareness of our Creator and pray: ...

● ● ●

•As we push aside the emotion of the mind and seek the peace in our hearts, we earnestly pray: ...

•As we take this time for renewal of our spirits, we pray:

● ● ●

•Let us stand and take refreshment from the practice of solitude and prayer: ...

● ● ●

•Let us each retire inwardly and become refreshed by the Fountain of Life as we offer words of praise and thanksgiving to our Creator: ...

• • •

•As we step aside from the tangles of life and take repose in our own inner sanctuary, we gain peace through the act of prayer: ...

• • •

•As we enter into the rhythm of soothing peace, we allow our minds to become still and reflect on these words: ...

• • •

•As we take this moment to be in touch with the Divine, we pray: ...

• • •

•Let us still our minds and open our hearts to our humble words of prayer: ...

• • •

•As we still our minds and rise to that place of silent knowing Thou art ever with us, we pray: ...

• • •

•As we remove our attention from outside influences, we spend this thoughtful moment in loving prayer: ...

• • •

•As we join together in stretching toward Reality, we pray: ...

• • •

•We are privileged today to renew our faith through prayer.

• • •

•May our minds become passive and receptive to our words of prayer.

• • •

●Let us contemplate on the higher nature of Spirit.

● ● ●

●May the living ardor of Spirit be with us as we pray: ...

● ● ●

●As we turn our attention to the deeper meaning of life, we earnestly pray: ...

● ● ●

●As we unite in a higher order of consciousness, we humbly pray: ...

● ● ●

●Let us take this moment to make contact with the deeper realities: ...

● ● ●

●As we bow our heads and poise our minds on the spaciousness of eternity, let us pray. We pray Dear Heavenly Father: ...

● ● ●

●Let us take this time for surrender to that ethereal place and pray: ...

● ● ●

●Dear God: May we become open and receptive to Thy all-pervading presence: ...

● ● ●

●Let us take this time to retreat from the roughage of daily living and pray: ...

● ● ●

●As we stand in honor and in adoration of Thy spirit, we pray:

● ● ●

●As we switch our attention from the mundane to the mystical place in our higher nature, we pray: ...

● ● ●

•As we turn inward and become receptive to a higher state of consciousness, we pray: ...

•••

•As we take this moment to call upon our higher soul nature, we humbly pray: ...

•••

•As we stand in loving attention, we make contact with the spiritual essence within our hearts.

•••

•Let us retreat to that quiet peace that passeth all understanding, as we pray: ...

•••

•Let us now break away from the disparity of existing conditions in our personal life and national problems and take on the rich refreshment of prayer: ...

•••

•As we shut out the intruding random thoughts, we become receptive to this moment of prayer:

•••

Invocations

SHORT INVOCATIONS
Dear God:

We thank You for this opportunity of meeting together. May we, through the stimulating association this membership affords, be dedicated to the service of our fellow man. We are grateful for the love displayed here and the strength and encouragement we gain from one another. We ask infinite guidance in all our efforts.

Give, we pray, peace, strength and wisdom to us. Bless our country and all the people of the world. Amen.

•••

Our heavenly Father:

We thank You for this privilege of meeting together in friendship and purpose. We are grateful that we live in a country where we may interchange ideas, pursue our ideals and speak without restraint.

We ask Your divine guidance for this meeting, for the leaders of our country and for all the people of the world. Amen.

•••

Lord, we gratefully accept our work, not as a daily grind, but as a daily accomplishment — a step to increased pride in purpose. Please bless this meeting with Your infinite love and wisdom. Guide our every action. Let us with all the people of the world be securely free from fear, through increased spiritual understanding and unwavering faith in Your divine plan for this planet's ultimate good. Amen.

•••

Dear God:
We ask for Your indwelling presence and blessing at this meeting. We know, like mirrors, that we are outwardly only a reflection of our inner self. Help us to reflect love and understanding to all.

Let the light of each spirit glow with the joyful enthusiasm of working, playing and praying together. Free us of discordant thoughts and lead us with love to take correct actions as needed here today. Let us be ever mindful of this privilege of meeting together with the freedom to speak our thoughts and to grow in stature through knowledge obtained from other speakers. Bless, we pray, these faithful members and their families. Peace to our world. Amen.

•••

Dear God:
As we meet here in search of knowledge and self-improvement, may we open our hearts to the love surrounding us. Help us to see individual growth, and keep our minds dedicated to learning, so that we can gain that "pearl of great price," wisdom.

We ask that each member take from this meeting a thought, an idea, a spark that will ignite and send light to others, thereby not only helping ourselves but our fellow men. We thank you for the love we have to share.

Bless these members, their families, our country and all the people of the world. Amen.

•••

Dear Father:

We are grateful for a life to live and a love to share. We also thank You for a faith that gives us the courage and understanding to adjust to our constantly changing world. We ask Your blessing on this meeting, in which we come together, motivated by unselfish purposes and generated by dedication to glowing ideals. Please grant that each gain fellowship through this association and reap inspirational benefits. Let us be ever mindful of the needs of people throughout the world. We ask divine guidance for all. Amen.

•••

Dear God:

Help us to know that the future cannot be measured by the past. Instill within each of us a technique for learning to live today with faith and expectancy, so that each day may be filled with unlimited opportunities. Help us to forge ahead to conquer new horizons. We ask Thy infinite wisdom, courage and strength to lead us in achieving individual and organizational goals. Allow us the privilege to be of service to others and to contribute, in some small way, to the seedling of peace and goodwill that is needed so desperately throughout the world. Amen.

•••

Dear Father:

We thank You for the blessings of this meeting and for all the benefits we derive from this association. Guide us in the exchange of interests, ideas and inspirations. Let us ever be aware of the power of faith, the presence of love and the purpose of knowledge. Grant, we pray, peace and understanding to all. Amen.

•••

Dear God:

We know that men must ever stretch themselves or shrink from inertia. May we not rest on past laurels, but set our sights on even higher plateaus of achievement. We ask that Thy guidance give us the direction, and that our faith in Thee renew our courage and willpower.

Please bless this membership as we give grateful thanks for the privilege of serving. Let us always remember to honor the rights of all men. We pray Thy grace be with the United Nations and the leaders seeking peace among nations and a world free from fear. Amen.

●●●

Invocations w/ Scriptures or Quotations

"Be not deceived; God is not mocked; for whatsoever a man soweth, that he shall also reap." (Galations 6:7)

Dear God:

As we enter into this time of communion with our brothers, united in spirit and dedicated to our mutual cause, we ask that Thou direct our efforts to the swift accomplishments of our goals. May we receive and be receptive to our creative urges, so our thoughts and actions be in harmony with Thy will. Give us, we pray, the inspiration and initiative to follow through on all our plans, for we know full well that "almost" is never enough.

Let us rest confidently in the knowledge that behind every seed endeavor is the life force for its perfect fulfillment. When we give our attention to only the "single eye" and envision the completed task, all doubt is erased from our minds. Only a mushroom reaches maturity overnight. Help us have the patience to watch our idea-plant grow to blossom and ripen in due season.

When we know that our accomplishments will benefit our fellowman, we gain strength and courage to carry our banner ever onward to reap a rewarding harvest.

Bless our absent members. May they join us in the celebration of service to our fellow man.

We pray for peace in our hearts and for peace in our troubled world. By keeping the high watch ourselves, we do our part to calm the storms of disorder. Amen.

•••

Paul told the Corinthians, *"Behold, now is the acceptable time; behold, now is the day of salvation."* (*II Corinthians 6:2*)

We must believe in and invite God into our actions and into our lives and affairs.

Dear God:

We trust this beautiful Gospel message and accept that now is the moment of the hour. Help us discard fogs of doubt and look with a clear vision into that infinite storehouse of self and pluck faith, self confidence, integrity and pride of endeavor into our hearts. These are the soul qualities... the very essence of our being. We ask that Thy infinite wisdom direct us to unmask greed and polish the armor of righteousness.

Thank you for the salvation of "now."

Bless our planet Earth and all its peoples. Amen.

•••

"Whatsoever things are lovely... and of good report... think on these things."

Dear Lord: As we turn our thoughts from the mundane daily duties and take a minute's refuge in our spiritual nature, we automatically "think on things of good report."

We trust in life and a universal plan of right action. Help us call forth the deep spiritual qualities of faith, hope, love and joy and spread them to our fellow man. When we recognize our unity, our sense of separateness is dissolved and we become royally elevated in stature. Bless us as we strive for that high estate. We give grateful thanks that we are inspired to work toward the alleviation of pain and suffering. Guide our way in this worthy endeavor.

May Thy presence be with the leaders of all the nations in the world. May they place world peace uppermost in their hearts and minds. Amen.

William James said, *"The greatest use of life is to spend it on something that will outlast it."*

Dear God:

We, too, want to make a lasting contribution to this community and its youth, and, perhaps as a consequence, a profound influence for good on the world.

We give grateful thanks for this opportunity. We ask Thy divine guidance in these endeavors. May the thoughts of our head and the works of our hands and the motives in our hearts be acceptable to Thy sight.

We fervently pray that peace, love and understanding be established on earth, so our children and theirs will not know the torments of fear. Amen.

● ● ●

As we quiet our minds, let us reflect on the words of George Bernard Shaw: *"What I mean by a religious person is one who conceives of himself or herself to be the instrument of some purpose in the universe which is a high purpose."*

Dear Lord:

We thank You for the privilege of meeting together in friendship to fulfill a high purpose by joining together in pursuing the noble tenets of our organization.

Pray, grant us the strength and courage to utilize our god-given talents to perform the tasks we have charted. Let our hearts swell with the soul satisfaction we gain by helping others.

Please bless the officers of our association as they devote their time and efforts to the common good.

May the leaders of our country and the leaders of the world be open and receptive to Thy divine wisdom, and sincerely seek ways to promote a permanent peace so all people can live free from fear. Amen.

Mahatma Gandhi (1869-1948) said: *"All the power I may have comes from God. But He does not work directly. He w orks through His numberless agencies."*

Dear God:

Let us be one of those numberless agencies to do Thy work. We give grateful thanks for the favor that You have bestowed upon us by allowing our interests to become centered in giv-ing aid to our fellow man. With Your unfailing guidance, we will prosper the thing to which we put our heart and hand. May Your grace be with us to fortify our inner strength and bring our outer actions to fruition.

We ask Your blessings on this membership and their families. Please send Your healing rays to those absent because of illness.

We remember always to include a request for peace and prosperity for all the people of the world, so hunger and strife will vanish from this earth. O Lord, please hear our prayer. Amen.

•••

"We, each of us, are a distinct part of the essence of God and contain a certain part of Him in ourselves."

—*Epictetus*

Dear Lord:

We have an instinct for joy that is our divine heritage — the child within all of us is still close enough to call. Let us call with faith that joyful, beneficent up-lifting spirit of joy.

When we put the presence of joy into our endeavors, we make small the effort and great the results.

In this moment of silent submission to a higher order, we ask You to fill our hearts with joy and let our heads and hands work in perfect harmony.

We give thanks for this opportunity to meet to pursue our common purpose. Grant that our strength, courage and dedication remain steadfast in the face of all challenges.

We ask Your blessings on this troubled world, and we pray that peace for all nations shall come to pass. Amen.

•••

Dear God:

We give thanks that we can meet today without fear of censure, and that we can speak without restraint. Thy ever-loving presence is our refuge and strength.

As we raise our minds to a higher estate, we ask guidance and wisdom in fulfilling our appointed objectives. We ask that the spark of inspiration be instilled in the hearts of each member. We are grateful for the opportunity to serve our fellowman and become a beneficent hand in our community.We ask that blessings of health and harmony be bestowed upon this membership and to those who are unable to be with us today.

In these tumultuous times, our fervent prayer is for divine order, peace and understanding for all races and creeds throughout the world. Let us take comfort in the words of Isaiah: *"So shall my word be that goeth forth out of my mouth: it shall not return unto me void, but it shall accomplish that which I please, and it shall prosper in the thing whereto I sent it."* (Isaiah 55:11) Amen.

•••

Dear God:

As we meet here today to take hold of our appointed tasks, we ask Thy guidance in all our undertakings. Let us each be attuned to our divine inner inspiration so we may become a channel for decisive right actions.

Keep our faith uplifted in the knowledge that back of every seed idea is its perfect fulfillment. Help us remove all doubt barriers from our mind and see with the "single eye" the accomplishments of our goals.

As we join together in our unified purpose, we ask that our efforts serve and benefit our fellow man and the world community.

Grant us the wisdom, strength and courage to carry us to a rewarding harvest.

We let Thy words ring in our hearts, *"Do not be deceived; God is not mocked, for whatever a man sows, that he will also reap."* *(Galations 6:7)*

• • •

Dear God:

As we take this moment to pray, we offer thanks for our plentiful gifts. We remember that there are others not so fortunate as we are. May our capacity to love be expanded to embrace all people in our love-hungry world. We pray that strife, fear and injustice to man be abolished from the face of the earth.

Please impart to us Thy spiritual wisdom so that we may perform Thy will with love and dispatch.

We lighten the heaviness of hearts by sharing our ideas, time and talents with others. We measure up when we reflect joy in our faces, creating a happy atmosphere.

Help, we pray, our officers as they take on the assignments charged them. Be with this membership, be with our absent members and fulfill their individual needs.

May we always walk with bold courage and unfaltering faith to show forth Thy glory. We hear Thy words... *"Ask and thou shalt receive."*

Amen.

• • •

General Invocations

Dear God:

We thank Thee for this day of infinite privilege to meet together and renew our dedication to the high principles the founders of this organization bequeathed us.

We ask Thy eternal blessings on our undertakings, that they may be accepted in the spirit of love and goodwill. The sharing of our time and energies is not performed as a duty, but for the fulfillment of our soul nature to aid our fellowman. May our moral standards be lofty and we stand proudly confident that our role in this organization is serving Thy divine plan.

We pray that our officers be given the wisdom and guidance to conduct affairs without heaviness of heart. When we pull together as one, it lightens the effort.

Please be with our absent members, meeting their needs.

We hold high hopes that the leaders throughout the world will open their hearts to tolerance and understanding for the betterment of all mankind.

Amen.

•••

Almighty God:

Grant us wisdom, so that we may ever be mindful that all we have emanates from You, and through that realization, learn to share the boons we enjoy with the less fortunate. Teach us, O God, to be grateful and contented amidst our failures and disappointments.

May the work of righteousness be peace, and the effect of righteousness, tranquility and security forever. Amen.

—*Rabbi Sidney S. Guthman*

•••

Dear Father:

As these beloved members meet to share the fellowship of each other and renew our dedication to our common goals, we ask for Thy wisdom in charting the course for achievement. As a mushroom does not reach maturity overnight, grant us the patience and follow-through necessary for success in our undertakings.

We pray that the spirit of peace and tranquility reign over this assembly, and that it flows out to all our absent members. Bless our families who give us their loyal support. Teach us to appreciate the worth and value of each person we touch. We know we are all of the same spirit and have an individual significance without equal.

Let our hearts be filled with compassion for the deprived and needy of our country and all the peoples of the world.

May all the world leaders be open and receptive to Thy divine guidance in the performance of their heavy tasks. May their prayers, along with ours, be that peace will be established in all the nations of the world.

Thank you for the multitude of blessings we so casually take for granted. Surely goodness and mercy shall follow us as we embark on our appointed duties. Amen.

• • •

Dear Lord:

We are grateful for this association and the opportunity it brings us to be a beacon of hope in our community, as we listen to the words of Henry Drummond: *"You will find, as you look back upon your life, that the moments that stand out are the moments when you have done things for others."*

Let us take humble pride and soul satisfaction in the past accomplishments, while we plan even greater undertakings. We ask that Thy invisible shield of protection be always with us.

With Thy divine guidance and wisdom, we are confident of success and give grateful thanks for the courage and faith instilled in the hearts of this membership.

May Thy enduring tenderness be with our absent members, and those who are in need of Thy solace and comfort.

We ask Thy special blessings on the leaders of our country. May they, with all the leaders of our world, be guided by divine right actions, with peace among nations uppermost in their minds.

Teach us, we pray, to do all things proceeding from love, with love as our true motivation. Amen.

●●●

Dear God:

We are grateful to be able to pause for this short devotion, which captures our restless attention and refreshes the inner depths of our soul nature.

These meetings bless us with cherished friendships, for which we give thanks.

We ask Thy divine guidance to make intelligent decisions in all our undertakings.

Help us set aside prejudices and see behind blind traditions of issues, social, political and economic, that are unworthy of our support. May we discern the real nature of one another as beloved children of the universe, a recognition that removes all hint of bigotry and hypocrisy from our minds and hearts. Let our love and compassion be awakened in full measure.

Please accept our gratitude for the fountains of blessing You have so lovingly bestowed upon us.

Be with our world leaders in their attempts to resolve the unrest of all nations. Our special prayers are with the United Nations in its effort to bring global peace. Amen.

• • •

Dear Lord:

We are grateful for this time when we can earnestly give thanks for our many blessings, those seen and not seen. We ask Thee to constantly make us more aware of the benefits this association brings into our individual lives in terms of unity, friendships and spiritual qualities of Faith, Hope, Love and Joy.

May we be empowered with insight and guidance to perform our tasks with an unwavering confidence and in a light-hearted manner. Help us seek harmony and balance on all levels of our life: business, family, social and fraternal. We put our trust in Thee.

Grant, we pray, the healing of those members who are in need of well-being because of physical ailments or mental perplexities.

Receive our fervent prayers that peace throughout the world be established among nations and in the hearts of all people.

Amen.

●●●

Lord:

As we still our minds and become open to that magnificence of our inner chamber in prayer, we acknowledge the boundless blessings Thou has bestowed upon us.

This association and the friendships fostered here is a treasure of measureless value, for which we give our heartfelt thanks.

Let us pay tribute to our officers, who perpetuate this organization and willingly dedicate their time and energies for the common good.

As we work together to further our service to the community, let us not forget to inject joy in our projects. Joy adds new zest and vitality to all endeavors and deepens our sense of purpose. Nehemiah said, *"The joy of the Lord is your strength."*

We ask divine guidance for all our undertakings, for Thy grace is our sufficiency.

May Thy enduring tenderness be with our absent members and those who need a special healing. We ask that solace and comfort be established unto them.

We pray Thy love and light surround the world to make a lasting peace possible in our time. Amen.

•••

Dear Lord:

As our beloved members come together to unify our ideas and thought to our common purpose, we humbly ask Thy sanctions on this meeting.

Let us remember the words of the wise Chinese philosopher who said, "A journey of a thousand miles begins with a single step." We ask that we take these steps light-hearted and not become mired down in the mud of discouragement. Guide us, we pray, for success in all our undertakings.

Please bless our absent or infirm members who we hold close to our hearts in brotherhood. May they rejoin our group with renewed strength.

We send thoughts of love to all the peoples of the world and ask that the dove of peace encircle our beautiful planet.

Let us not forget to thank you, God, for the beauty and bounties of nature and for the joy of living. Let us learn each day to grow in knowledge and understanding. Amen.

● ● ●

Dear God:

We are blessed in innumerable ways with benefits from this association. The sharing of ideas and ideals lends an added dimension to our lives. We thank Thee for this opportunity.

Love, hope, faith and courage, royal qualities so earnestly admired, cannot be manufactured. They are gifts from Thy infinite storehouse.

We ask for guidance to purify our heart and expand these spiritual faculties. Enrich our innate instincts to display unconditional love for our fellow man and hold fast to a creed of a reverence for life.

Give us confidence that we can bring our many talents into visible manifestation, and thereby become a blessing to those who need our services.

Please be with those members who are ill and want the comfort of our joint prayers for healing.

May we all become as one in our dream and desire for world peace, so our children and their children will know Utopia on our beautiful planet, Earth.

Amen.

•••

Dear Lord:

As this meeting is called to order to join in harmony with the principles of our organization, we ask that each member share their thoughts, ideas and inspirations with the group, so we may become a strong, cohesive unit for the fulfillment of our immediate and long-range goals.

Success in any undertaking often is judged by the obstacles. We ask that we make molehills rather than mountains of any we may encounter. With divine guidance, we are confident that our tasks will be illumined by candles of success.

We give thanks for Thy presence and blessings on this meeting. May those members unable to attend know that they are with us in spirit.

Our hearts go out to all the leaders of our cities, states and nation. We pray that they be open and receptive to Your word.

Help us each to hold high, lofty thoughts for world peace.

We give grateful thanks for grace and blessings. Amen.

• • •

Dear Lord:

We offer grateful thanks for Thy presence at this meeting.

May the purpose and principles of our organization be diligently upheld by our actions. We pray for Thy unfailing guidance.

Knowing that love is the divine creative force that animates all life, we request that we become living streams of love pouring it to all, especially to those with drooped shoulders and heavy hearts.

As we become immersed in the bustle of our service activity, let us not forget that feelings of joy will make our tasks lighter.

May Thy blessings be with us and our absent members.

Grant, we pray, wisdom to the leaders of our country and to the leaders of races throughout the world.

Hear, O Lord, our urgent prayers for peace and understanding among all people on this beautiful planet, Earth.

Amen.

•••

Dear Father:

Bless our meeting and uplift our thoughts so that we may communicate with each other from an infinite depth of deep understanding.

Give us the wisdom of allowing each member to give the special gifts and talents that are uniquely theirs. When our motives are pure and we give without the thought of receiving praise or recognition, we truly bestow treasures from the heart.

Help us remember that a good receiver is as vital to the scheme of life as an unselfish giver. Let us enjoy the fruits of being on both sides.

We give grateful thanks for the friendships this association offers us, and the inspiration we get from each other.

May Thy universal blessings encircle the globe, so that all men and women throughout the world will experience the comfort of a peace that passes all understanding.

Amen.

•••

Lord:

Let us in this moment of communion lay down our anxieties, lay down impatience and frustration and seek the calming comfort of Thy presence.

When we still our minds of frantic effort, our true goals can come into focus and we can in prayer humbly ask that Thy grace be with us in the performance of our business.

We ask that Thou destroy the negative doubt weeds from our minds and plant positive, healthy seeds that will become sturdy plants and flourish, so we become a garden of hope for all who need our assistance. Let us not forget, "not our will, but Thine, be done."

Bless our dedicated officers. May Thy spirit guide them as they successfully carry out their duties.

Be with our absent members. We ask a special blessing for those who are in ill health.

May Thy divine wisdom be with the leaders of our country and the leaders of all nations, so they put spiritual vigor into promoting peace on earth.

Amen.

• • •

Dear God:

As we meet together, we ask that Thou remove all restraints and limitations from our minds that could compress us into pygmies in the jungle of doubt. Help us to rise to the stature of giants in the pursuit of our mutual goals.

As we view the stars and the planets moving in their fixed orbits in harmony with the universal plan, so too, we ask for divine guidance in perpetuation of our noble organization.

We offer grateful thanksgiving for the love and loyalty of this membership. May each person take from this meeting a divine impulse to satisfy their inner longing for spiritual awareness. Through this fraternal unity, an untold measure of blessings will manifest in our lives.

As we allow our spiritual "sonship" to be reborn, we pray that the efforts of our hearts, head and hands be of benefit to our fellowmen.

Dear God, as we awaken our consciousness to the work ahead, let us hold foremost in thought our prayer for world peace. May the dove of peace descend to circle the globe. Amen.

●●●

Dear God:

As we meet here today to rededicate ourselves to the high principles of our organization, let us remember that we do not have to live up to the standards of others, but to those standards of our own conscience. The virtures of honesty and integrity are firmly implanted in our innermost being. We can walk uprightly when we place them at the top of our agenda.

Please bless the causes of our assocation. May we take pride that we can be of service to each other and to our community. By doing our full share, we help lighten the heavy load of world despair.

We thank Thee for this opportunity to be spiritually fulfilled with the higher innate qualities of life: love, faith and joy. May joy and peace always reign in our hearts.

Bless us and all the people of the world with understanding and trust. Amen.

•••

Dear God:

As we meet here in search of knowledge and self-improvement, may we open our hearts to the love surrounding us. Help us be grateful for the cherished friendships this association fosters. As we unite in our joint efforts to support each other in reaching our individual goals and take pride in all accomplishments, we fulfill a deep spiritual need to be of service. We humbly ask that this meeting be meaningful to the membership and that each of us capture a thought, and idea, a spark that will ignite and produce a light that will brighten our lives and the lives of others.

We thank You for the love we have to give and to share.

Bless these members, their families, our country and all the peoples of the world. Amen.

•••

Dear God:

We ask Thy guidance in upholding the high principles that are the foundation of our organization and in putting those principles and goals into action.

Help us fully appreciate the joy of bonding-friendships this association offers and the enrichment to our lives in the self-satisfaction of being of service to our fellow man.

Let us hold high the torch of love, charity and tolerance for all to see.

Bless this membership, we pray, and all those who are missing from our ranks, because of illness or other reasons.

May Thy gift of love enfold all the peoples of the world so freedom from fear, and peace and tranquility may be established on our beautiful planet. Amen.

● ● ●

Dear Lord:

We ask that Thy blessings be bestowed upon these devoted members as we seek to be a measure of hope for those who are downcast and feel the pangs of hopelessness.

We pray that the love of moral justice become uppermost in the hearts of all mankind, so this world will become a better place in which to live.

May Thy grace be with us and guide us to the fulfillment of our appointed duties.

Grant, we pray, that love, wisdom and understanding be instilled in the minds of the leaders of all countries, that they become leaders for peace on our planet Earth. Amen.

● ● ●

Our heavenly Father:

We beseech Thee to bestow Thy blessings on this meeting. We are grateful for our abundance of material and spiritual gifts, and for the fellowship this association affords us by enlarging our scope of living. We ask Thy infinite guidance in all our undertakings, that we may grow in wisdom and understanding, thereby benefiting our society.

It is with a deep sense of pride that we are mindful of the privilege we have to meet without fear, to openly listen, to form our own decisions and to speak without restraint.

May Thy grace be with our absent members, and may our loving concern hasten a recovery if needed.

We pray Thy love will encircle our globe and will lighten the heavy hearts of people throughout the world. Amen.

• • •

Dear God:

As we meet together today, may we experience the joy of true companionship and sharing ideas to further our association's ideals.

Even though life sometimes seems to be a mystery, we are grateful we can turn to You for direction and guidance. We ask that divine wisdom be with us as we progress on our path of appointed tasks. Help us to the perfect fulfillment of our goals.

We pray that Thy loving hand is accepted by all the nations in the world as we strive for freedom from fear and total peace for all humanity. Amen.

• • •

Inspirations — Poems and Prose

(Refer also to the Appendix "Resources: Where to Find It.")
An inspiration is a stimulus that lights an "Ah-ha" in our head and injects a love dart in our heart; that raises us from the mortal self to a higher realm, stretching heavenward for eternal values. Art, music and words have a profound effect on our lives. Prose and poetry written to express illumined feelings can inspire the reader or listener to a more sublime state of mind.

Today, our libraries are filled with the spiritual wisdom of the saints, sages and poets throughout the ages, and we have access to the treasure chest of knowledge of the prophets of the past and present. Truly, a new age in the history of mankind.

The following are samples you may wish to use at your meeting when you are called upon to give an inspirational discourse.

Peruse other chapters in this book for additional material.

A DAY WORTHWHILE

I count that day as wisely spent
In which I do some good
For someone who is far away
Or shares my neighborhood.

A day devoted to the deed
That lends a helping hand
And demonstrates a willingness
To care and understand.

I long to be of usefulness
In little ways and large
Without a selfish motive
And without the slightest charge.

Because in my philosophy
There never is a doubt
That all of us here on earth
Must help each other out.

I feel that day is fruitful
And the time is worth the while
When I promote the happiness
Of one enduring smile.

—Thanks to an unknown author

THE WINDING WAY

We climbed the height by the zigzag path
And wondered why — until
We understood it was made to zigzag
To break the force of the hill.

A road straight up would prove too steep
For the traveler's feet to tread;
The thought was kind in its wise design
Of a zigzag path instead.

It is often so in our daily life;
We fail to understand
That the twisting way our feet must tread
By love alone was planned.

Then murmur not at the winding way,
It is our Father's will
To lead us Home by the zigzag path,
To break the force of the hill.

—*Thanks to an unknown author*

LIFE'S SPLENDOR

Forget each kindness that you do
    as soon as you have done it.
Forget the praise that falls to you
    the moment you have won it.
Forget the slander that you hear
    before you can repeat it.
Forget each slight, each spite, each sneer
    wherever you may meet it.
Remember every kindness done
    to you, what e'er its measure.
Remember praise by others won
    and pass it on with pleasure.
Remember every promise made
    and keep it to the letter.
Remember those who lend you aid
    and be a grateful debtor.
Remember all the happiness
    that comes your way in living.
Forget each worry and distress;
    be hopeful and forgiving.
Remember good, remember truth,
    remember Heaven's above you,
And you will find through age and youth,
    true joys and hearts to love you.
It's the giving and doing for somebody else —
    On that, all life's splendor depends.
And the joys of this life, when you sum them all up
Are found in the making of friends.

—Author unknown

COUNT BLESSINGS

There are always two sides,
    the good and the bad.
The dark and the light,
    the sad and the glad —
But in looking back over
    the good and the bad,
We're aware of the number
    of good things we've had —
And in counting our blessings
    we find when we're through
We've no reason at all
    to complain or be blue.
So thank God for good things
    He has already done.
And be grateful to Him
    for the battles you've won,
And know that the same God
    who helped you before
Is ready and willing
    to help you once more.
Then with faith in your heart
    reach out for God's Hand
And accept what he sends,
    Though you can't understand,
For our Father in heaven
    Always knows what is best.
And if you trust in His wisdom,
Your life will be blessed.

—Anonymous

THE POWER OF LITTLES

Great events, we often find,
On little things depend,
And very small beginnings
Have oft a mighy end.

A single utterance may good
Or evil thought inspire;
One little spark enkindled
May set a town on fire.

What volumes may be written
With little drops of ink!
How small a leak, unnoticed,
A mighty ship will sink!

Our life is made entirely
Of moments multiplied,
As little streamlets joining,
Form the ocean's tide.

Our hours and days,
Our months and years,
Are in small moments given.
They constitute our time below —
Eternity in heaven.

DO NOT JUDGE TOO HARD

Pray don't find fault with the man who limps
　　Or stumbles along the road.
Unless you have worn the shoes he wears
　　Or struggled beneath his load.
There may be tacks in his shoes that hurt,
　　Though hidden away from view;
And the burden he bears, placed on your back,
　　Might cause you to stumble too.
Don't sneer at the man who's down today,
　　Unless you have felt the blow
That caused his fall, or felt the shame
　　That only the fallen know.
You may be strong, but still the blows
　　That were his, if dealt to you
In the selfsame way at the selfsame time
　　Might cause you to stagger, too.
Don't be too harsh with the man who sins,
　　Or pelt him with words or stones,
Unless you are sure, yea, doubly sure,
　　That you have no sins of your own.
For you know, perhaps, if the tempter's voice
　　Should whisper as soft to you
As it did to him when he went astray,
　　'Twould cause you to falter, too.

—Selected

DESIDERATA

Go placidly amid the noise and haste, and remember what peace there may be in silence. As far as possible, without surrender, be on good terms with all persons. Speak your truth quietly and clearly, and listen to others, even to the dull and the ignorant; they, too, have their story! Avoid loud and aggressive persons; they are vexatious to the spirit.

If you compare yourself with others, you may become vain or bitter, for always there will be greater or lesser persons than yourself. Enjoy your achievements as well as your plans. Keep interested in your own career, however, humble; it is a real possession in the changing fortunes of time. Exercise caution in your business affairs, for the world if full of trickery. But let this not blind you to what virtue there is; many persons strive for high ideals, and everywhere life is full of heroism.

Be yourself! Especially, do not feign affection. Neither be cynical about love, for in the face of all aridity and disenchantment, it is as perennial as the grass. Take kindly to the counsel of the years; gracefully surrender the things of youth. Nurture strength of spirit to shield you in sudden misfortune. But do not distress yourself with dark imaginings. Many fears are born of fatigue and loneliness.

Beyond a wholesome discipline, be gentle with yourself; you are a child of the universe no less than the trees and the stars; you have a right to be here. And whether or not it is clear to you, no doubt the universe is unfolding as it should. Therefore be at peace with God, whatever you conceive Him to be; and whatever your labors and aspirations in the noisy confusion of life, keep peace in your soul. With all its sham, drudgery and broken dreams, it is still a beautiful world. Be cheerful. Strive to be happy.

—Old Saint Paul's Church, Baltimore. 1602.

God of life,
there are days
when the burdens we carry
chafe our shoulders
and wear us down;
When the road seems dreary and endless,
the skies grey and threatening;
when our lives have no music in them,
and our hearts are lonely,
and our souls
have lost their courage.
Flood the path with light,
we beseech Thee;
turn our eyes
to where the skies
are full of promise.

—St. Augustine

PERCEPTION
An Idealist looking upon a man
considers the grace
reflection
manifested of a heavenly face.

A Realist proclaims
a handsome beast,
amazingly bright,
but soon obsolete.

The Thomist cries praise
for what God has made
out of atoms, light
His omnipotence displayed.

The Pragmatist says
to work for today.
Tomorrow, who knows
we may decide to play.

The Existentialist sits
twisted over one shoe
contemplating, deciding
whats right he should do.

A Saint looks at man,
understanding his place;
working toward perfection
God's ordered fate.

—*Mimi Lozano (c)1971*

The disorder that surrounds us
which keeps us from our source
results from confused and empty values
in which we put our trust.

Reach for the center of endless time;
this be your inner drive,
finding joy in silent knowing
each moment is divine.
> —*Thanks to Mimi Lozano, (c) 1984, National*
> *League of American Pen Women*

● ● ●

TIME IS...
> too slow for those who wait
> too swift for those who fear,
> too long for those who grieve,
> too short for those who rejoice,
> but for those who love...
>> Time is Eternity.

● ● ●

SLOW ME DOWN, LORD

Ease the pounding of my heart by the quieting of my mind. Steady my hurried pace with a vision of the eternal reach of time. Give, me, amid the confusion of the day, the calmness of the everlasting hills.

Break the tensions of my nerves and muscles with the soothing music of the singing streams that live in my memory. Help me to know the magical, restoring power of sleep.

Teach me the art of taking minute vacations — of slowing down to look at a flower, to chat with a friend, to pat a dog, to read a few lines from a good book.

Slow me down, Lord, and inspire me to send my root deep into the soil of life's enduring values, that I may grow toward the stars of my greater destiny.

●●●

LOVE

There is no difficulty that enough love will not conquer;
No disease that enough love will not heal;
No door that enough love will not open;
No gulf that enough love will not bridge;
No wall that enough love will not throw down;
No sin that enough love will not redeem.
It makes no difference how deeply seated may be the
    trouble,
How hopeless the outlook,
How muddled the tangle,
How great the mistake,
A sufficient realization of love will dissolve it all...
If only you could love enough, you would be
the happiest and most powerful being in the world.

—Emmet Fox

To see the world in a grain of sand,
And a heaven in a wild flower;
Hold infinity in the palm of your hand,
And eternity in an hour.

—*William Blake*

● ● ●

If one should give me a dish of sand and tell me there were particles of iron in it, I might look for them with my eyes, and search for them with my clumsy fingers, and be unable to detect them; but let me take a magnet and seep through it, and how would it draw to itself the almost invisible particles by the mere power of attraction. The unthankful heart, like my finger in the sand, discovers no mercies; but let the thankful heart sweep through the day, and as the magnet finds iron, so it will find, in every hour, some heavenly blessing, only the iron in God's sand is gold.

—*Henry Ward Beecher*

● ● ●

Keep your faith in all beautiful things; in the sun when it is hidden; in the spring when it is gone... And then you will find that duty and service and sacrifice—all the ogres and bugbears of life — have joys imprisoned in their deepest dungeons! And it is for you to set them free — the immortal joys that no one — no living soul, or fate, or circumstance — can rob you of, once you have released them.

—*Roy Rolfe Gilson*

● ● ●

117

COMMONNESS OF LOVE AND LURE

Hurry not, dear stranger,
To reach your journey's end;
Pass not by the works of God
That commonness attends;
Be not deaf or blind to see
Loves and lures He made to be:

See the loftiness of trees
In a forest's pride;
See the quiet strength of brawn
In a mountain's side;
Smell the fragrance of the flowers,
Blooming by your way;
Listen to the woodland's brooks —
laughing, night and day;
Hear the happy songs of joy
Children sing at play;
Hear the melodies of life
All along your way;
Feel the freshness of the earth;
Feel the summer rain;
See the majesty of snow
Dress the barren plain;
Look to see the rising sun;
Breathe the air of dawn;
See the birth of evey day —
Where new hopes are born;
Touch the early morning dew;
Smell the new-mown hay;
Rapture in a twilight's hues
At the close of day.

Hurry not, dear stranger,
To reach your journey's end.
See the wondrous works of God
That commonness attends.
Tomorrow may not bless your way
With the gifts you own today.

—Michael Dubina

• • •

"Man is not the master of the universe because he can split the atom. He has split the atom because he first believed in his own unique mastery. Faith led to the material achievement, not achievement to the faith. In fact, now that the means of mastering the environment, of building — physically — a better world, are more complete than ever before,it is a paradox that the faith is slackening.

—Barbara Ward (From "Faith and Freedom")

• • •

GUIDEPATHS TO PEACE
Be glad of life because it gives you the chance
to love and to work and to play and to look up
at the stars; to be satisfied with your possessions
but not content yourself until you have made
the best of them; to despise nothing in the world
except falsehood and meanness, and to fear nothing
except cowardice; to be governed by your admirations
rather than by your disgusts; to covet nothing that
is your neighbor's except his kindness of heart and
gentleness of manners; to think seldom of your enemies,
often of your friends, and every day of Christ; and to
spend as much time as you can with body and spirit in
God's out-of-doors — these are the guidepaths to peace.

—Henry Van Dyke

119

MAKE A PEARL

Most of us can afford to take a lesson from the oyster. The most extraordinary thing about the oyster is this: Irritations get into his shell. He does not like them; he tries to get rid of them. But when he cannot get rid of them, he settles down to make of them one of the most beautiful things in the world. He uses the irritation to do the loveliest thing an oyster ever has a chance to do. If there are irritations in our lives today, there is only one prescription: make a pearl. It may have to be a pearl of patience, but anyhow, make a pearl. And it takes faith and love to do it.

—*Harry Emerson Fosdick*

• • •

CHOICE

Our lives are songs; God writes the words
    And we set them to music at pleasure;
And the song grows glad, or sweet or sad,
    As we choose to fashion the measure.

—*Ella Wheeler Wilcox*

• • •

Individualized Prayers

AFFIRMATIONS AND MEDITATIONS
Affirmation:

Various churches and devotional study groups regularly recite affirmations as part of their services. As affirmations are a very private type of prayer, meeting the needs of the individual at a particular time, group affirmations have been excluded from this book.

Samples of Affirmations:

Dear God:

I know that the pressures of everyday living often obscures my mental picture to a point that I do not always express a genuine love for others, because I am thinking more about my own feelings and not about theirs.

I ask now that my thoughts release personal affairs and transcend the daily cries of chaos in the news, allowing me inner peace and security, so I may transmit love and understanding directly from a pure heart, not contaminated by a muddled mind.

Please, God, let me be worthy of the supreme gift, the sumum bonum — unreserved love for all life! Amen.

• • •

...And now abideth faith, hope, Love, these three; but the greatest of these is Love. (I Corinthians 13:13)

• • •

OUR SPIRITUAL INHERITANCE

I am health, strength, peace, happiness and prosperity. The Spirit of God, which is active in me, flows through my physical body in a purifying, cleansing, healing stream that removes all obstructions and brings peace, health and harmony to my body.

I am well, strong and vital.

I am beautiful, peaceful, poised.

I am eternally youthful.

I am buoyant, happy free.

I shall arise in the morning filled with energy, radiance and the power to accomplish whatever I find to do.

—Unkown Author

•••

I am at the place of New Beginnings.

I stand in God's time — NOW — knowing my needs are met now; the need for provision, security, freedom, intelligence, wisdom, understanding, foresight, companionship and love — most of all love. I am companioned by love and appreciation, and all my needs are met now. There is no yesterday, no tomorrow, only NOW.

I am very still because I am conscious of God's presence, and I am listening for guidance. I know that I have a place to fill and work to do that is mine. Where is it? How do I find it? My desire is to be about my Father's business, where all my needs are met so abundantly because I am expressing the Love and Wisdom that created the universe. With God, all things are possible.

Yesterday's lessons learned: the problems, the joys and sorrows, the work I had to do, all slip away into the mists of the past, and I wait. I look around at the beauty and abundance of nature; the ceaseless activity; the freedom of the skies; the joyous exuberance of animals; their love and trust. Can I do less? I am overwhelmed with gratitude for the unlimited abundance that is mine — now — that nothing can take from me because they are the gifts of Divine Love.

Suddenly in the stillness, the answer comes. How? Perhaps a statement I have read or heard — perhaps the still, small voice within — or intuition. I only know it is my answer. If there is action to be taken, I do not let doubt or fear enter my thoughts as procrastination. If there is action to take I do it, knowing I know what and when and how to do, because I do not walk alone. I take the first step with confidence, knowing the others will follow, and my way is made clear before me — moment by moment in the NOW of God's time. And I give thanks and listen, and go forward.

—*Pauline Bush*

•••

And I give thanks and listen, and go forward. Thou art to keep thyself in this silence and open the door so God may communicate Himself unto thee, unite with thee, and then form thee unto Himself. The perfection of the soul consists not in speaking, nor in thinking much on God, but in loving sufficiently.

—*Miguel de Molinos (1640-1697)*

•••

123

MEDITATION

"Meditation: The art of suspending verbal and symbolic thinking for a time, somewhat as a courteous audience will stop talking when a concert is about to begin."

—*Alan Watts*

Meditation, in contrast to prayers, which often request God to intercede in a problem, is a contemplative type of communion with the Deity. Rather than talking to God, one is practicing "The Thunder of the Silence."

Instinct will act in jarring bedlam, whereas intuition breeds best in silence and meditative moments.

Instinct is a part of the subconscious mind, the mind that protects the animal organism from danger and attends to its physical needs.

Meditation is extending God the courtesy of being quiet, to allow intuition a space to enter the busy mind chamber.

Many churches practice a form of meditation during their service. The leader is not restricted to a prescribed length. The tone and type of meeting dictate its duration. The membership normally does not stand during a meditation. Often soft background music and lowered lights help contribute to the ambiance of the occasion.

As group meditation is generally conducted by professionally trained members of the clergy and students of different doctrines, I feel it is presumptuous on my part to include samples of this type of meditative ceremony.

Many religious bookstores carry beautiful meditation cassettes.

However, Pauline S. Clow, licensed practitioner and former inspiration chairman of the Leisure World Women's Club of Seal Beach, Calif., has generously volunteered her own personal meditation to be used as a sample in this chapter.

MY MEDITATION

"I sit early in the morning reading uplifting and spiritual affirmations, starting my day with treatment for myself, my loved ones and my clients. I experience a closeness and a nurturing of spirit.

"I go for my morning meditation walk, and I am aware of the freshness of the morning, the dew on the roses, the fragrances of the new day. Life expresses itself as rabbits, birds, trees, an auto and an airplane. The energy of the universe manifests the pulsation of life. As my feet move, one supporting the other, providing the ability for me to move forward on the path or in life is a miracle. I am aware of my heartbeat, alive with this same rhythm of the breath of life that has been provided for me. I greet a fellow walker who is experiencing life according to their individual acceptance.

"I return home to enjoy a freshly brewed cup of coffee. I am aware that the coffee bean was planted, nurtured and harvested, processed, shipped and reaching my table by many avenues that spirit traveled. I drink the coffee, eat the fruit and toast and ponder the paths that they traveled to

125

reach my table. How can the fruit and toast make hair and bones and give me energy for the moment?

"Spirit expressing in so many ways that I know not of, nor do I understand. I do not need to know how. All I need to do is to be aware and meditate with thanksgiving on any and all the beautiful blessings each day. Always there, always available. It is the Father's good pleasure to give me the kingdom! I am at choice to accept or reject.

"Meditation to me is being aware — being aware of life and life expressing individually for, through and as me. Yes, I am an individual expression of God. I express God according to my awareness and willingness to share in this moment, one moment at a time, knowing that the next moment may be experienced and expressed differently according to my awareness.

"My awareness is enhanced and expanded according to my acceptance. For me, meditation is to be — be aware!"

—Pauline S. Clow

Special Prayers
contributed by Notables

Almighty God:

At this opening of our meeting, we pray to you for a full measure of your wisdom and strength, that our two-fold heritage as Americans and Jews may be alive and meaningful within us. May the ideals of democracy continue to grow and develop in the world to bring blessings to all men. May the tradition and faith of Israel continue to enrich and ennoble our lives. Grant, O Heavenly Father, that our command ever be motivated by this heritage. In peace as in war, may we always be champions of righteousness and justice. Guide our deliberations and bless us, that we may bring closer to reality your kingdom upon earth, our vision and our goal through the ages. Amen.

—Cmdr. Caroline Staff,
South Coast Dist. of Jewish War Veterans

• • •

We pray, O God, that we will use the abilities that You have given us in ways that benefit others and bring a measure of justice and mercy to what we do. We ask your forgiveness when we miss the mark and when we do not act as the people you would have us be. May your precious spirit so touch our lives and the lives of every person, that good works will flow from our hands, respect for others will be our standard, and kindly words will be the indication of our love. This is our prayer. Amen.

—The Rev. James David Ford, D.D.
Guest Chaplain to the House Of Representatives,
Washington, D.C.

127

Let us pray:

"Thou shalt love the Lord thy God with all thy heart, and with all thy soul, and with all thy mind. Thou shalt love thy neighbor as thyself. On these two commandments hang all the law and the prophets. (Matthew 22:37,39,40)

Almighty God, as election campaigns heat up, anger grows, cynicism deepens and emphasis seems to be placed on personality rather than issues. Somehow, gracious Father, help us hear the word of God, that "love is the fulfilling of the law." We accept the diversity endemic in democracy and the healthy dynamics of a two-party system, but deliver us from attitudes and actions designed to destroy opponents. Help us heed the wisdom of a wise man, the late Rev. Vance Havner, who said, "The foundations of this country were not laid by politicians running for something, but by statesmen standing for something!" And grant grace to those in political battle to cool it.

We ask this in the name of Jesus, the Prince of Peace who incarnated love. Amen.

—The Rev. Richard C. Halverson, D.D.
Chaplain to the U.S. Senate, Washiington, D.C.

● ● ●

Heavenly Father:

We ask you bless our nation and its people. May our ties of fellowship and citizenship be strengthened. Protect us from all catastrophes and disasters. Unite us in peaceful struggle toward true progress and prosperity; may it become reality through the productive work of all.

Send your blessing upon all those responsible for the destiny of this nation. Grant the representatives of the people the strength and courage to make decisions for the well-being of all. Help them to preserve the climate of freedom, justice and opportunity for all in this great nation.

Protect all citizens; encourage them in their efforts during these difficult times in the cities and rural areas, along the borders and on the world scene, and thus help build a happy and beneficial future for all our citizens. Amen.

—The Rev. Tom Hargesheimer,
St. Pius X, Rochester, MN
Guest Chaplain, House of Representatives
Washington, D.C.

● ● ●

O God of grace and God of glory:

When we resent having so many choices to make, may we remember that good character is the habit of choosing right from wrong.

Help us, as a nation, to see that our strongest defense lies back in home and school and church where is built the character that gives free people that power to win their freedom and to hold it. May we never forget that it is only under God that this nation or any nation can be free.

And when we have learned well this lesson, then shall we have for export more than money, even the faith and idealism for which all who love liberty will be willing to live. Amen.

—Peter Marshall

• • •

Our Father, who art in Heaven:
Where we are wrong, make us willing to change, and
where we are right, make us easy to live with.

O Lord our God... save us from accepting a little of
what we know to be wrong in order to get a little of
what we imagine to be right.

Give us clear vision that we may know where to stand
and what to stand for - because unless we stand for
something, we shall fall for anything.

Forgive us, our Father, for taking our good things for
granted, so that we are in danger of losing the fine art
of appreciation... make us grateful for the bounties
we enjoy that we shall try, by Thy help, to deserve them
more.

Deliver us, we pray Thee, from the tyranny of trifles.
May we give our best thought and attention to what is
    important, that we may accomplish something worth-
while...

teach us how to listen to the prompting of Thy spirit, and
    thus save us from floundering in indecision that wastes
time...

and multiplies our troubles.

—Peter Marshall
Former Chaplain, U.S. Senate

● ● ●

Dear God:

Help me be a good sport in this game of life. I don't ask for
an easy place in the line-up. Just put me where you need me.
I'll only ask that I can give you 100 percent of all I have. If the
hard drives seem to come my way, I thank you for the
compliment. Help me remember that you never send a player
and have him do more than he can handle. Help me, O Lord,
to accept the bad breaks as part of the game. And may I always
play the game on the square no matter what the others do. Help
me study the books so that I can know the rules. Finally, God,
if the natural turn of events go against me and I am benched
for sickness or old age, please help me to accept that as part of
the game, too. Keep me from whimpering or squealing that I
was framed or that I ruined a deal. And when I finish the final
inning I ask for no laurels. All I want is to believe that in my heart
I played as well as I could. Amen.

—Cardinal Richard Cushing

CHAPTER 8
Good Graces

•Table Blessings

CHAPTER 8
Good Graces

TABLE BLESSINGS

Grace is a message to the infinite expressing gratitude for material blessings and may be delivered before or after the meal. It usually is related to food and thanksgiving, although the purpose of the meeting may be mentioned briefly. The most common custom is to say any grace prior to the meal. In instances where some tables have been served and the guests are eating, it would be awkward to interrupt, and a prayer of thanks may be said afterward.

This delivery should be reverent and very short. The membership may sit or stand during this presentation.

Although an inspiration may be given at luncheons and banquets, the grace message is the generally accepted presentation. If the inspiration is chosen, it should not be lengthy and allow the food to cool.

GRACES WITH SCRIPTURES

"And the Lord will guide you continually, and satisfy your desire with good things." (Isaiah 58:11)

Dear Lord:

We thank Thee for the good things this sterling occasion has to offer in the way of nourishment to our bodies, minds and hearts. Please bless us. Amen.

•••

Dear God:

We ask that Thou be with us as we partake of this meal. May this social outlet also be a spiritual inlet.

"We give thanks to thee, O God; we give thanks; we call on Thy name and recount Thy wondrous deeds." (Psalms 75:1) Amen.

•••

"For where two or more are gathered together in my name, there am I in the midst of them." (Matthew 18:20)

Dear God:

We give thanks for Thy presence and the high level of love consciousness displayed at this banquet. Please bless our food and the membership. Amen.

•••

Dear God:

We ask that Thee bestow Thy blessing on this meeting for the food which is to be served. This is an occasion of celebration and rejoicing. We read in scriptures: "I give thanks to God always for you because of the grace of God which was given you in Christ Jesus." (I Corinthians 1:4) Amen.

•••

"And taking the five loaves and the two fish he looked up to heaven, and blessed, and broke the loaves...and he divided the two fish among them all. And they all ate and were satisfied." (Mark 6:41-42)

We thank Thee, Lord, that our abundance comes not only from this meal, but also from the fellowship this sharing occasion creates. We ask Thy eternal blessings be on these members and their families. Amen.

• • •

"This is the day which the Lord has made; let us rejoice and be glad in it." (Psalms 118:24)

And may we also rejoice that we have this opportunity to break bread together and share the fellowship of this occasion. Thank you, God, for our many blessings. Amen.

• • •

"He who supplies seed to the sower and bread for food will supply and multiply your resources and increase the harvest of your righteousness." (II Corinthians 9:10)

Dear God:

We thank Thee for the friendships fostered here and the harvest of blessings in our lives. Amen.

• • •

"For everything created by God is good, and nothing is to be rejected if it is received with thanksgiving." (I Timothy 4:4)

And we do take time to accept this meal with thanksgiving knowing that it will nourish our bodies and the fellowship will nourish our hearts. Thy grace is our sufficiency. Amen.

• • •

"Let us come into his presence with thanksgiving." (Psalms 95:2)

As we join together in this hour of social communion, we renew our faith in the source of all our blessings. We give thanks for this meal and for all the benefits and pleasures it affords us.

Dear Father:

May we express our gratitude to Thee in bringing us together to break bread and share our qualities of spirit and distinct personalities with one another. May this time of sociability be a blessing for all in attendance. And, *"Thanks be to God for his inexpressible gift!"* (II Corinthians 9:15)

• • •

"He brought me to the banqueting house, and his banner over me was love." (Song of Solomon 2:4)

And we accept the love which abounds in this room as we enjoy this meal that affords us untold blessings. Thank you God.

• • •

BRIEF GRACES
Dear Lord:

Goethe said there would be little left of him if he were to discard what he owed to others. As we partake of this meal and the companionship it affords, let us remember to be grateful for our debt to you, for infinite love and for our caring members, who add an extra dimension to our lives. Amen.

• • •

As we join together to give thanks and partake of this food, may we realize that this sustenance is not the real requirement for our well-being. Our zest, motivation and energy are derived from each other. We are grateful for this association and its material and spiritual benefits to us.

Thank you, God. Amen.

• • •

Dear God:

We ask Thy ever present love on this meeting. We give thanks that we may be together and break bread together and be surrounded in harmonious friendships. Amen.

• • •

Carlyle said, *"Our grand business is not to see what lies dimly in the distance, but to do what lies closely to hand."* And as our food is about to be served, let us pause for a moment in prayer to give thanks for the meal and the fellowship we are about to enjoy. Thank you, God, for all our multitudinous blessings. Amen.

• • •

We ask God's blessing on this meeting. May we have the strength, courage and faith to handle our business affairs in the loving fashion we display at these luncheons. We give thanks for this food and fellowship. Amen.

• • •

We ask God's ever-present love on this assembly. And we give grateful thanks that we take this time to be together, and eat together in a bond of friendship and harmony. We'll not forget to thank you, God, for our many blessings. Amen.

• • •

Dear Lord:

We ask that Thou bless our food. And may we take the joy of this occasion with us into our world of affairs, so we may become beacons of light for Thy works. Thank you for our many-fold blessings. Amen.

• • •

Dear God:
We ask Thy infinite love bless this meeting, and the food which we are about to eat. The joy we share at these occasions nourishes our hearts, minds and bodies. We give thanks for this opportunity. Amen.

•••

Dear Father:
Please bless us as we meet and dine together. May we be married in ideals, divorced of hypocrisy and gain inner contentment by working together in harmony, with the same conscious acceptance and firm beliefs we have instilled within our hearts when we pray together. Thank you for this food and all its benefits. Amen.

•••

Dear Lord:
We know that the joy in our hearts is reflected in our eyes. May we keep that bright sparkle as we join in dining together at this happy occasion. May Thy love reign throughout our meal and be with us eternally. We give thanks for all our many blessings. Amen.

•••

We thank you God, for the nourishment of love, hope and faith that feeds our soul, the friendships that comfort our hearts, and for this food which gives sustenance to our bodies so we may live meaningful lives. We ask your grace, guidance and blessings on this assembly. Amen.

•••

As we are about to dine, let us realize that we do not live in a vacuum; that we all have something to give to others. May we, in this social moment, give a bit of ourselves, so that all may benefit from this meeting. Thank you, Father, for this food and its blessing. Amen.

• • •

Dear Lord:
We thank you for the abundant blessings bestowed upon us. This food is but a symbol of Thy eternal care. The love and fellowship displayed here keeps us aware of Thy presence. Amen.

• • •

Dear God:
We ask Thy blessing on this special occasion in which we come together not only for a social repast but for the enrichment of our minds. May Thy grace be with our speaker today and with the membership. We give grateful thanks for the food and the spiritual benefits this meeting offers us. Amen.

• • •

Dear Father:
Make us perceptive to all abundance and responsive to all good. We ask Thy blessing on this meal and our meeting. Amen.

• • •

CHAPTER 9
Close with Blessings

- Benedictions

CHAPTER 9
Close with Blessings

BENEDICTIONS

A benediction is a blessing that often concludes a meeting. Although it is said at banquets and social affairs, it more commonly is used to end a religious service.

Many church study groups close meetings with a benediction, as it can lend a spiritual, inspirational or fraternal tone to the parting courtesies. Some organizations use a "closing thought" to conclude their meetings.

Brief is the word for benedictions, but one need not be as brief as the Army chaplain during World War II who received national acclaim through his cries by the trenches, "Praise the Lord, and pass the ammunition!"

There is no set format in the wording, length or delivery. Generally it is short, but how short depends on the kind of meeting.

In a general business meeting with a set time frame, the membership may not fully appreciate a lengthy benediction in their haste to leave on schedule — brief is better. Tailor the benediction to meet the need.

If a benediction is to follow the meeting, that item of business should be listed on the program. When there is no program, the presiding chair may wish to announce the concluding event before the last speaker, so the audience is prepared to sit for that extra minute before adjournment — especially if a benediction is not a regular custom at the general meetings.

Because a benediction may not necessarily be a communion with God, the "Amen" may be omitted and a "good night," "good day" or "good afternoon" substituted. "Amen"—"May it be so" or "So it is"—is used after prayer to express approval.

A sampling of various styles are presented in this chapter. You can also use these examples as a starting point to formulate your own benediction.

Benediction (Webster's Dictionary):
1. *A blessing or the act of blessing.*
2. *An invocation of divine blessing, usually at the end of a service.*

Dear Lord, may Thy transcendent presence be with us as we depart from this meeting. We pray each member take a gem of insight with them and may peace be with them until we meet again. Amen.

• • •

Dear God: Let us like the captain at sea, in the face of all storms, remain courageous and confident in the unseen powers for divine guidance to our safe harbor. Amen.

• • •

Dear Lord: May Thy invisible shield of protection be with each member as we depart from this meeting, until we meet again. Amen.

• • •

Lord: As we leave this meeting, let us stand boldly under the wings of the Almighty and be ever grateful for His protective grace.

• • •

146

Dear God: As this meeting is dismissed, so should we dismiss our belief in temporal power and renew our faith in the supernal goodness of Thy infinite power. Amen.

• • •

May the love and joy fostered at this meeting follow us until we meet again.

• • •

We ask that God's grace guide and bless each of us as we go our separate ways and bring us safely back to our next meeting. Amen.

• • •

Dear God: It has been said, "It is better to give than to receive." We here give thanks that so many of these members are willing to give their time to this organization. May they receive the joy of inner satisfaction in their admirable achievements. We pray all those in attendance receive Thy blessing as they go forth from this meeting. Amen.

• • •

Dear God: As we go from this meeting filled with love and thanksgiving, we ask that Thy blessings be upon all the peoples of the world and that each person will know the joy of serenity from a peaceful heart. May Thy grace go with us. Amen.

• • •

Dear God: The joy of sharing is not a commodity to be measured, but it is the "pearl of great price." We are grateful for the many pearls in this organization. Grant, we pray, peace and fulfillment to these dedicated members and their families. Be with us until we meet again. Amen.

• • •

Dear God: May Thy blessings follow this membership as we leave this meeting with joy and thanksgiving that we have accomplished that which was before us. May peace be with us all until we meet again. Amen.

•••

As we go forth from this meeting, may we take the spirit of comradeship, the joy in serving and the radiance of God's love with us as our constant companions, until we meet again. Amen.

•••

As we depart from this meeting, may we hold the shield of faith steady before us to be our protecting armor in the days that follow. May God bless us in all ways. Amen.

•••

As we bask in the glory of Thy spirit, protected and guided, we go forth into a new hour with joy and thanksgiving for God's ever-present presence. Amen.

•••

As we part from this meeting, let us each feel the all-enveloping love our Creator surrounding us and our loved ones. May God's grace be always with us. Amen.

•••

May God grant perfect peace, health and happiness to you and yours until we meet again.

•••

Dear Lord, may the friendship displayed at this meeting be repeated throughout the world. God grant peace, joy, love and understanding to all people. We pray His blessing go with you until we meet again. Amen.

•••

Dear Father, as we adjourn this assembly, may each person be blessed with the inner joy of a job well done. We are grateful for the fraternity this organization offers and the opportunity to share time, talents and ideas toward a common goal.

Bless all of us as we go forth from this meeting, and give us a safe journey home. Amen.

• • •

Because God is our sustenance, our security and our salvation, we go forth from this meeting free from fears of the "terrors of the night" and abide in our unrelenting faith, that we will live by the still waters until we meet again. We give grateful thanks for Thy grace. Amen.

• • •

Dear Father: There is no joy more rewarding than the sharing of friendship, unless it be the joy of sharing in accomplishments. The hearts of this assembly should be filled and overflowing with a double joy. We ask Thy blessings for these members, their families and friends as we go forth from this meeting with the inner joy in "a job well done." Amen.

• • •

We ask that Thy grace be with us. May we know, as did Julian of Norwich in her moment of exalted revelation, gazing at the smallness of a hazel nut, *"The first is that God made it; the second is that God loveth it; the third is that God keepeth it."* Amen.

• • •

In closing, let us take to heart an Indian proverb: *"Until we meet again, may the Great Spirit make sunrise in your heart, and may your moccasins make tracks in many snows yet to come."*

• • •

As we go forth from this meeting, may the benefits continue to sharpen our minds and deepen our hearts. So, the rewards of our communion become immeasurable. May God's glory and grace go with us. Amen.

•••

As we adjourn this meeting with feelings of exaltation and joy, may we send our love to encircle the globe and include all races on earth. God's universal love is everywhere present, and as we open wide the portal of our hearts to receive it, we send it into the world. We ask that God's glory go with us. Amen.

•••

As we depart from this meeting, may our hearts and spirits stay glad, that we will meet again to pursue our joint goals for the benefit of our fellow-traveler on our beautiful spaceship Earth. We give thanks to God for the love fostered through this association and the opportunity to be of service. May God bless us. Amen.

•••

Before we rush through the exit gates, let us take a moment and reflect on the benefits we received from this meeting: the renewal of friendships, and the wealth of information imparted us by our speaker.

Dear God: We give thanks to these and many more blessings this association affords us. We ask that Thy loving presence be with these members until we meet again. Amen.

•••

Dear God: With the knowledge that we have gained from this meeting, may we put on spurs of resolution to help us perform admirably our appointed tasks. We ask Thy blessings accompany us as we adjourn from this assembly. Amen.

•••

Dear God: We give grateful thanks that we live in this period of time that we can meet freely and discuss without fear of censure the pressing problems of the day. We ask Thy blessing as we go forth from this meeting with a greater understanding. Amen.

•••

May God's blessings be with us as we leave this meeting with a head full of knowledge, a heart full of dedication and inspiration. We give thanks that we can be instruments in Thy service and a benefactor for the community. May our high resolve continue to spark our actions until we meet again. Amen.

•••

As we prepare to leave this meeting, let us say a prayer to God for the gift these speakers have brought us in terms of knowledge and inspiration. With their message still ringing in our minds, let us listen to the profound words of Paul, who, when in captivity and chained to a Roman soldier, gave this message to the world:

"Finally, brethren, whatsoever things are true, whatsoever things are honest, whatsoever things are just, whatsoever things are pure, whatsoever things are lovely, and of good report; if there be any virtue, and if there be any praise, think on these things."

•••

With the close of this meeting, may we take with us the nuggets of truth expressed here and put them into use in our daily life. We give grateful thanks for our speakers and their inspiring messages. May God walk at our side and bless us eternally. Amen.

•••

151

"Who seeks for heaven alone to save his soul may keep the path, but will not reach the goal; while he who walks in love may wander far, yet God will bring them where the blessed are."

—Henry Van Dyke

May we be blessed until we meet again. Amen.

•••

"We shall steer safely through every storm, so long as our heart is right, our intention fervent, our courage steadfast and our trust fixed on God."

—St. Francis De Sales

And as we depart, we place our trust in the Almighty. Amen.

•••

"Life is divided into three parts — that which was, which is, and which will be. Let us learn from the past to profit by the present, and from the present to live better for the future."

—Wordsworth

Let us walk in love until we meet again. Amen.

•••

"No man has a right to lead such a life of contemplation as to forget in his own ease the service due to his neighbor; nor has any man a right to be so immersed in active life as to neglect the contemplation of God."

—St. Augustine.

As we adjourn, we ask that God's blessing be with us until we meet again. Amen.

•••

Henry Wadsworth Longfellow said, *"We judge ourselves by what we feel capable of doing, while others judge us by what we have already done...."*

As we go forth from this meeting, we can take sincere pride in our accomplishments — a job well done! We thank you, God, for Thy presence. May Thy spirit be with each of us until our next meeting. Amen.

••••

Albert Schweitzer said, "*The creative force, which produces and sustains all that is, reveals itself to me in a way in which I do not get to know it elsewhere... as something which desires to be creative within me.*"

Thank you, God, for the blessing of the creative spirit in this membership. The rewards of being productive have no limits. Please be with us as we depart from this meeting with the prideful satisfaction of true accomplishment. Amen.

••••

In 428 B.C., Plato said, "*This kind of knowledge is a thing that comes in a moment, like a light kindled from a leaping spark which, once it has reached the soul, finds its own fuel.*"

Dear Father, we give grateful thanks for the fuel we have received from this meeting. May our flame of inspiration burn brightly until we meet again. Amen.

••••

Henry Drummond said, "*You will find, as you look back upon your life, that the moments that stand out are the moments when you have done things for others.*"

Dear God, we ask Thy blessings on these dedicated members as they go forth from this meeting with the assurance that the moments spent together in service pursuits will long be remembered by the beneficiaries of our time and efforts. And if, perchance, we remember these moments as highlights in our life, we will be the wealthiest in rich memories. Amen.

••••

153

George Bernard Shaw said, *"What I mean by a religious person is one who conceives himself or herself to be the instrument of some purpose in the universe, which is a high purpose."*

Dear God: We thank you that through this organization we become instruments for a "high purpose." We ask your protective presence be with this membership and their families for eternal time. Amen.

●●●

Thoreau said, *"Be not too moral. You may cheat yourself out of much life, so aim above morality. Be not simply good, be good for something."*

Dear God: We thank Thee for this meeting and for this organization that affords us the best of both worlds, morality and being and doing "good" for others. Bless these members as we take leave of this assembly. Amen.

●●●

Let us take these comforting words from the scriptures as we leave this meeting:

"He who dwells in the shelter of the Most High... will say to the Lord, My refuge and my fortress; my God, in whom I trust. "(Psalms 91:1,2) Amen.

And with the promise of freedom from fear we part, until we next convene. May God bless us all.

●●●

"I am not alone, for the Father is with me. I have said this to you, that in me you may have peace." (John 16:32-33)

And with the confident words from John we depart with God's blessing. Amen.

• • •

"You will be secure, and will not fear. You will forget your misery; you will remember it as waters that have passed away. And your life will be brighter than the noonday." (Job 11:15-17)

Dear God: That is our prayer until we meet again. Amen.

• • •

"God is love; and he that dwelleth in love dwelleth in God, and God in him." (I John 4:16)

May each of us dwell in love until we meet again. Amen.

• • •

Dear God: With a heart full of thanksgiving for the fraternal love displayed here at this meeting, we claim our unity with Thee from the words of the Scriptures:

"So then you are no longer strangers, and sojourners, but you are fellow citizens with the saints and members of the household of God." (Ephesians 2:19)

• • •

With the blessings we have received from this meeting, we will take still another as we listen to a promise from the Bible.

"Be strong and of good courage, do not fear or be in dread of them: for it is the Lord your God who goes with you; he will not fail you or forsake you." (Deuteronomy 31:6)

May God bless each and every one of us. Amen.

• • •

155

Some churches use this "Prayer for Protection" to conclude their meetings:

"The light of God surrounds us;
The love of God enfolds us;
The power of God protects us;
The presence of God watches over us;
Wherever I am, God is!"

•••

As we each go our separate ways, let us put our faith in the Almighty.

"Whither shall I go from Thy spirit?
Or whither shall I flee from Thy presence?...
If I take the wings of the morning
    and dwell in the uttermost parts of the sea,
Even there Thy hand shall lead me,
And Thy right hand shall hold me."(Psalms 139:7-10)
We give thanks for the security of God's hand. Amen.

•••

As we close this meeting, may we be reassured by the comforting words: *"Fear not, for I am with you and will bless you."* *(Genesis 26:24)*

•••

May the words of the scripture be our sanctuary:
"Be strong and of good courage... for it is the Lord your God who goes with you; he will not fail you or forsake you." (Deuteronomy 31:6)

•••

As we leave this meeting we take solace from words of the Scriptures, *"Whither shall I flee from Thy presence?" (Psalms 139:7)*
We give humble thanks for this infinite security. Amen.

•••

156

CHAPTER 10
Special Events

- Conventions and the Club Chaplain
- Holidays and Patriotic Observances
- Nationally Recognized Birthdays and
  Commemorative Days
- Invocations for Specialized Groups and
  Meetings

CHAPTER 10
Special Events

CONVENTIONS AND THE CLUB CHAPLAIN

Conventions are the culmination and the celebration of another cycle on the association pattern — an exciting, fun time for the membership, and hopefully for the convention coordinating team. After months of preparation—sometimes years — planning for this gala highlight event, it does not always follow the blueprint.

The maze of details involved in playing host to large numbers of people can be overwhelming. Taking people out of their native element and transporting them to an unfamiliar area and arranging housing, meals and entertainment is an undertaking that could strain even Sampson or Solomon. Despite this, there are thousands of conventions every year.

Fortunately, many hotels and convention centers employ personnel to help organize the affair. Even so, the host city and the club convention committee accepts a great responsibility, a monumental task that may take one's nerves to task. Stressful situations occur no matter how well-planned the operation.

Some wise sage once said, "If you try to please everyone, you won't accomplish anything — and if you do please everyone, you're not doing it right!"

At a recent convention, a delegate walked up to the chairman and said, "I want to offer some constructive criticism."

The coordinator smiled and said, "Oh, I'm sorry, but that department won't be open until after final adjournment. Why don't you just say, 'I love you'?" With that, she gave the would-be complainer a big hug. She made not only a friend, but a devotee, who followed suit by passing out hugs.

As chaplain and an ambassador of goodwill, you can assist the convention committee by keeping a smile on your face and declaring, "Everything is wonderful!" Inject words of praise whenever possible. Often, you will find that anytime a positive statement is made in opposition to a negative one, the topic will be dropped. How does one respond to "But, I thought it was wonderful!"

A testimony to harmony is never out of order. Even in the midst of noise and clamor, if one person is projecting an aura of inner balance, it may soothe a scattered situation.

In any event, if you keep your spirits buoyed and display a joyful attitude, your radiance will infect others. A spread of the joy virus never needs an antidote.

Complaints about food seem to reap more than their share of down-lip service. Perhaps it's natural, because no one cooks like mother.

As chaplain, you may want to give a boost to the chef and the convention facilities while saying a grace message to bless the food. And a silent prayer that you don't have to eat your words.

Here's an example of a grace blessing to compliment the chef:

Dear Lord:

Let us remember that Thanksgiving is not just the third Thursday in November. Thanksgiving represents a season of harvest. Nature abounds with visible evidence of this season making ready for a new cycle. Animals gather seeds and nuts for the next period, the tree completes the ring to its trunk and is ready for another.

This convention is our thanksgiving harvest, and we are here to begin a new cycle and to share what we have reaped with one another.

We are grateful that this host city and this facility are welcoming us in such a warm manner and the food services are displaying loving care in these high-quality meals to help sustain our bodies.

We give thanks and ask Thy blessing on this food and this convention. Amen.

• • •

At conventions, banquets and other large gatherings, the use of a microphone is advisable for the blessing service. The chaplain need not be seated at the head table, but must be prepared to reach the microphone in an unobtrusive manner. Struggling through crowded aisles or weaving through a maze of tables may bring giggles from the audience and break the solemnity of the occasion.

An introduction into the prayer may help still any unsettledness in the assembly.

An invocation at a convention may be longer than at a stated meeting. Therefore, the presiding officer will make the decision on whether the audience should stay seated or stand. When the salute to the flag follows the prayer, it is smoother to ask the membership to stand for the blessing.

At banquets where it is customary to use only the shorter grace message, the audience usually remains seated.

When you are choosing material for your convention prayers, bear in mind the purpose of the convention and try to include a sentence that includes these goals. The reasons for a convention may include formation of new policies; electing new officers; passing resolutions; recognizing outstanding achievements; or cementing cohesiveness within the organization.

But perhaps the most important feature of a convention is the fraternal friendships and fun experiences shared by delegates and members. This point could be emphasized in your prayer presentation. It also would be gracious to include the dedicated efforts and hospitality of the host chapter or city.

Here are some samples that can be altered to meet individual needs:

CONVENTION INVOCATIONS

Our Father:

We ask the divine nature within each person to be awakened to the full realization of the privilege this convention affords us, to be of service to others.

It is with eager expectancy that we anticipate greater understanding, cementing of friendships, finding joy in our work together, and the spiritual and material gains offered.

We realize that "sweetness" is not always in the attainment of set goals, but also in the challenging work necessary to bring about complete fulfillment of those goals.

We ask Thy blessing and guidance for this meeting. Let us each be sparked with enthusiasm, gain inspiration and grow in spirit as a result of our association.

May each of these leaders and delegates take back to their membership the true significance and strong purpose of this organization, along with the unblemished beauty of a priceless picture for their memory book.

Grant peace to all the peoples of the world. Amen.

● ● ●

MEMBER/DELEGATE RECOGNITION

Dear God:

We ask Thy blessings on this assembly. Many have traveled long distances to attend and have donated their personal time and money to help make this convention a success. We pray Thy divine guidance will be with us as we make the decisions to perpetuate and further the objectives of this organization. May each delegate receive the knowledge and inspiration they seek to help their home chapter be fully informed on the actions and goals of their national headquarters.

Let us remember to take our work seriously, and also our playtime, because it is in our social affairs that we gain a bonding in spirit and fraternal friendships are created. Please keep our faith in ourselves and our fellow man strong, for it is through faith in Thy unfailing presence that we gain the strength and fortitude to "move mountains."

Help us recognize that transient world affairs need not drag down our spirits, and that we help lift heaviness by keeping high hopes for freedom from fear. May Thy light of love and understanding burn brightly in the hearts of all mankind. We earnestly pray for peace. Amen.

●●●

CONVENTION COMMITTEE RECOGNITION

Dear Lord:

We are indeed blessed by the attendance of all these delegates, who so unselfishly donate time and expense to further this association's worthy causes.

Help us accept our assignments with light hearts, so no friction becomes apparent despite the massive details of this undertaking.

We ask Thy special blessings on the convention committees. May they be spiritually fulfilled by the satisfaction of a job well done.

The welcome the host city has afforded us is beyond measure. A simple "thank you" seems inadequate.

We ask Thy grace and guidance be with us as we attend to the successful operation of this convention.

Please give us the strength and courage to carry through to complete the set goals of our agenda.

We give grateful thanks for this opportunity to make new friendships and share in the work and play this occasion offers.

May Thy wisdom be with us in the days that follow. And, we pray that we each may contribute our small part of love, understanding and compassion toward peace and goodwill to our world. Amen.

•••

NEW OFFICERS

Dear God:

We are constantly reminded of Your unfailing benevolence to us in countless ways. We share this privilege of being together on this joyous occasion, when we pay homage to the outstanding leadership of our past officers. We offer loving loyalty to the new officers who have graciously accepted the helm of this organization. The unselfish donation of their time is without measure. We ask that they be guided by Your divine wisdom to make their "yoke easy and their burden light."

Please bless these members. May they return to their homes with renewed enthusiasm and dedication to the high principles and goals of this organization.

We are grateful for the friendships fostered by this convention. May the fraternal love displayed here put forth the hand of brotherhood to all in need.

We pray Your omniscient wisdom be with all the world leaders and bring peace to all humanity. Amen.

●●●

ACHIEVEMENT

Dear Lord:

We give grateful thanks for this opportunity to honor those members whose outstanding achievements have made us proud. We are indeed blessed by sharing in the joy of this occasion. And we also thank you for this organization, which made this award celebration possible.

Help us hold true to the high principles of this association, so that we become a blessing to our cause and to others in the community.

We pray Your guidance and wisdom be with these officers and members as they return to their respective chapters to fulfill the obligations we have pledged to support at this convention.

We ask Your protection be with them for a safe return.

May peace, love and understanding swell in the hearts of all mankind. Amen.

●●●

Dear Father:

We ask for your indwelling presence and blessing on this meeting. We know that, like mirrors, we are outwardly only a reflection of our mind, heart and soul. Let us reflect only love and understanding to all. Let the light of each spirit glow with the joyful enthusiasm of working, playing and praying together during this convention. Free us from any discordant thoughts, so that only love and right action prevail throughout this session. Let us be ever mindful of this privilege of meeting together without fear, speaking without restraint and growing in stature through knowledge. We thank you for these blessings. We ask harmonious right action, through divine guidance, for our meeting. May each member take home a fresh thought, a new idea or inspiration that will add a measure of value to their lives.

We ask that Your light and love give comfort to all the peoples of the world. Amen.

• • •

Father:

We are grateful for this opportunity of meeting together. We are thankful for these dedicated members and officers. We reverently ask Your blessing and guidance for our meeting. We know there is no limit to what men can do if they care not who gets the credit. We are not working for credit, but for good — so we know our actions and ideas and goals are divinely directed and God-inspired. We pray for strength, courage and wisdom to bring these desires to fruition. May each member receive a share of spiritual and material gifts from this meeting.

We humbly ask Your peace and blessing for all the peoples of the world. Amen.

• • •

Dear Lord:

We know that we have the same measure of time — 24 hours a day — and we are free to use this time to our individual liking. That is why we give grateful thanks for these dedicated delegates who have seen fit to give their time and effort to our common purposes and goals. Please bless each and every one present, and all the many throughout the country who are with us in spirit. Give us the wisdom to meet the needs of each member. Grant, we pray, divine understanding, love and courage to all the peoples of the world. Amen.

●●●

Our Heavenly Father:

We are constantly reminded of Your goodness and the divine spark within each of us that desires complete fulfillment of our purpose in life.

We are thankful for this opportunity to meet together, to be of service and act on behalf of our co-workers across the nation. We ask Your divine guidance in all our undertakings.

Grant us and the lawmakers of our country strength, courage and wisdom. Keep us united in spirit, thought and deed.

We pray for peace throughout the world. Amen.

●●●

*Pledge of Allegiance
to the Flag*

*

I pledge allegiance
to the flag
of the United States
of America
and to the Republic
for which it stands,
one Nation *under God,*
indivisible, with liberty
and justice for all.

Holidays and Patriotic Observances

"Holiday" derived from "holy day," is a day set aside by law or custom for the suspension of business, usually in commemoration of some event.

The President of the United States or Congress cannot declare a "national holiday," for each state has jurisdiction on the date of observance. Proclamations and public laws passed pertaining to holidays by our national legislators affect only the District of Columbia and federal employees. The various states must ratify the dates the holidays are to be observed by other than federal employees in those states.

A synopsis prefacing selected holidays is included for organizations that hold special ceremonies to commemorate American holidays.

PATRIOTIC HOLIDAYS

Although specific designations have been labeled on some of the invocations and inspirations in this section, you may find that the message also is appropriate — for instance, Flag Day and Independence Day. Mix, match or take out of context, according to your needs and taste.

May: Armed Forces Day*
May: Memorial Day **
June 14: Flag Day
July 4: Independence Day
November: Veterans Day **

*Third Saturday
**Monday holiday law

I LOVE AMERICA

I love America,
From sea to surging sea,
She is my place of birth,
My own nativity!
I love her mountain peaks,
Her fields of golden grains,
Her ranches and her farms,
Across the fertile plains!
I love America,
Her canyons steep and grand,
Her miles and miles of roads
That stretch across the land!
I love her busy towns,
The homes where millions live,
The people of each state
Who have so much to give!
I love America
Her oceans and her seas,
Her rivers and her parks,
Her giant redwood trees!
I love each church and school
From East to thriving West,
She is my home, sweet home,
The land I love the best!

—Nona Keen Duffy
Former member, National League
of American Pen Women

ARMED FORCES DAY

The third Saturday in May was named Armed Forces Day by Presidential proclamation in 1947 by Harry S. Truman. This was to replace Army Day, April 6; Navy Day, Oct. 27; and Air Force Day, the second Saturday in September.

Although Armed Forces Day is not a legal or public holiday, it is observed in military establishments and in many localities with appropriate ceremonies.

On May 21, 1960, President Dwight D. Eisenhower announced from the White House:

"It is America's hope and purpose to work continually toward the peaceful adjustment of international differences, and it is fitting that Armed Forces Day again emphasize the fact that our strength is dedicated to keeping the peace."

At another Armed Forces Day ceremony, he said that this time is to be "devoted to paying special tribute to those whose constancy and courage constitute one of the bulwarks guarding the freedom of the nation and the peace of the free world." The Chief Executive appealed to state executives and private citizens to display the Stars and Stripes "to show their recognition of the gallantry, sacrifice and devotion to duty of the men and women of the armed forces."

•••

Whatever your task, work heartily, as serving the Lord. (Colossians 3:23)

•••

"The fate of unborn millions will now depend, under God, on the courage and conduct of this army...."

•••

Dear God:

We thank you for those beautiful heroes of the past who proved to us, their beneficiaries, that liberty is synonymous with life. And though they put the initial stamp of will and desire on freedom, it is our duty to continue with vigilance to guard and defend our rights for our time and for the generations to come. Our hearts swell with pride in the servicemen and women in this country, the veterans and enlistees who individually rose above the spur of self-ambition to that higher inner impulse to serve this nation.

We salute those who willingly put God and country on the pedestal of worship and chose the path of love and service for all Americans and for humanity, so the forces of good will prevail throughout our world.

We pray these guardians of peace accept our prayers in their behalf as our small contribution of our debt of gratitude. Dear Lord, we ask Thy blessings and grace go with them in fulfilling their duties in the military and as private citizens.

May the leaders of our country accept Divine guidance and use their leadership power only for the welfare of our planet and all its inhabitants.

We thank you, God, for this opportunity to express our thanks to all the Armed Service personnel of this United States of America. God bless them. Amen.

● ● ●

MEMORIAL DAY

This day is set aside to remember our fallen heros of past wars and conflicts, who gave their all in the service of our country. We owe them a debt of gratitude, but that is not to say that we use this day for tears and mourning. That act would be an unbecoming tribute to our valiant veterans.

We keep sacred the memory of all sons, daughters, sisters, brothers, neighbors and friends who aided the cause of liberty for their country. We honor and praise them for their dauntless deeds. This also is a day in which we pay homage to our own loved ones who have passed beyond the veil of our limited vision.

Foods, costumes, music and customs from the "old country" become diluted with each new generation. In retrospect, this is a shame, because the distinct flavor of a nationality adds enhancement to our culture. No stew will reach the perfect state until the conglomeration of vegetables and spices have been put into the pot and allowed to simmer. America's diversity of religion and cultures could be the mysterious ingredient of this country's strength of will-power, and failure to follow a pattern of individuality may weaken the character fibers of our nation.

Appreciation and recognition of cultural differences does not lessen unity of spirit on patriotic or moral issues. These universal qualities create a cohesive bond, which in essence is the heartbeat of the American way of life.

Like remnants of the past, we often accept a holiday without knowing its background and history. Memorial Day, a very symbolic and patriotic holiday, has a beginning worth repeating, so future generations will not consider it only a picnic and wiener-roast celebration.

At a recent Memorial Day ceremony, Caroline Staff, Commander of Jewish War Veterans, Post 175, read the proclamation of John A Logan, Commander in Chief of the Grand Army of the Republic during the Civil War.

"On this day, the solemn tread of marching feet resounds through the cities and hamlets of these United States, as men and women of goodwill pay tribute to our valiant dead and renew our pledge of allegiance to the country for which they gave their earthly lives.

"Memorial Day is now a national holiday, but it began as so many of our holidays have begun, with a kind of unselfish gesture by simple people whose hearts were gentle and forgiving.

"In a quiet little Mississippi town, two years after the Civil War had ended, a group of women took fresh spring flowers up to their cemetery as a tribute to their men in gray.

"When the women had left the cemetery... it was found that they had placed the flowers... not only upon the graves of their heroes, ... but also upon the graves of those who had worn the Union Blue. As word of this touching tribute swept through the North, it stirred, as nothing else could have... national unity and love.

"Then, in 1868, Memorial Day was proclaimed a national holiday by General Logan's Memorial Order, which in part states:

"Headquarters, Grand Army of the Republic Washington, D.C.

May 5, 1868

1. The 30th day of May, 1868, is designated for the purpose of strewing with flowers or otherwise decorating the graves of comrades who died in defense of their country during the late rebellion, and whose bodies now lie in almost every churchyard in the land. In this observance no form of ceremony is prescribed, but posts and comrades will, in their own way, arrange such fitting services and testimonials of respect as circumstances may permit.

"We are organized, comrades as our regulations will tell us, for the purpose, among other things, "of preserving and strengthening those kind of fraternal feelings which have bound together the soldiers, sailors and marines who united to suppress the late rebellion."

"What can aid more to assure this result than by cherishing tenderly the memory of our heroic dead, who made their graves with sacred vigilance.

"Let no wanton foot tread rudely on such hallowed grounds. Let pleasant paths invite the coming and going of reverent visitors and fond mourners. Let no vandalism of avarice or neglect, nor ravages of time, testify to the present or to the coming generations that we have forgotten the cost of a free and undivided republic.

"Let us, then, at the time appointed, gather around their sacred remains and garland the passionless mounds above them with choicest flowers of springtime; let us raise above them the dear old flag they saved from dishonor.

2. It is the purpose of the commander in chief to inaugurate this observance with the hope that it will be kept up from year to year.

"He earnestly desires the public press to call attention to this order, and lend its friendly aid in bringing it to the country in time for simultaneous compliance therewith."

by command of
John A. Logan
Commander in Chief

N.P. Chipman
Adjutant General

Today, Memorial Day includes the fallen veterans of all battles. Individuals use this day to honor the memory of loved ones, friends and neighbors now deceased.

Memorial Day will always be a special day to those who have felt the heart-sick loss of a loved one. In deference to our faith, we try not to make it a somber occasion, but only a reverent celebration of tribute that may pacify a hidden hurt in our hearts.

OUR FLAG

How dear to my heart is the Star Spangled Banner
The banner our comrades fought bravely to save,
Many a dear lad gave his life to defend it,
And sleeps his last sleep in a faraway grave.
We cannot forget what it cost to preserve it;
The blood that was spilt — the tears that were shed.
The anguish endured — when the names of our loved ones
Appeared on the list, wounded, missing or dead.
The Star Spangled Banner we hold as a treasure
The banner that floats without blot, without stain
The Star Spangled Banner we love beyond measure;
The banner baptized in the blood of the slain.
There's a mission; Old Glory, before thee
The oppressed, the downtrodden, all over the world,
Are waiting, and watching, and longing to see
The emblem of freedom forever unfurled.

—Leona Talbott

Dear Lord:

Let us so live that the light of love in our hearts be rekindled and transmitted to others who secretly cry for an affectionate embrace. May the ring of infinite love from our Creator be perpetuated from those of the past to the present, thereby fulfilling the holy admonition to love one another.

As we are like mirrors, each person reflects a glimpse of inner truth about ourselves. We offer grateful thanks for the self-knowledge others teach us, and we humbly ask that we be given the wisdom to learn from the past, live in the present and love unconditionally.

Dear Lord, we ask Thy blessing on this meeting, and may Thy comfort steady those with faltering hearts.

"Because thy steadfast love is better than life, my lips will praise thee." (Psalms 63:3) Amen.

● ● ●

FLAG DAY

Out of the travail of our nation's birth, in the midst of a bitter war for independence, there emerged on June 14, 1777, our national emblem, a beautiful flag combining the blue of vigilance, perseverance and justice with the white of purity and the red of hardiness and valor in a symbol of freedom that has lifted the hearts of Americans down through the years.

It has been said that our Stars and Stripes is a "living" flag. It breathes vitality as it ripples in the breeze. It has exemplified vigor and endurance in proclaiming man's freedom and his right to life, liberty and the pursuit of happiness through almost two centuries.

It grows as our nation grows, adding a star for each new state taken into our Union.

On June 14, 1777, Congress passed the flag resolution:

"Resolved that the Flag of the United States by 13 stripes alternate red and white; that the Union be 13 stars white in a blue field, representing a new constellation."

That our flag sprang from an idea of Washington, rendered into immutable fact by Betsy Ross, is purely legend. As often happens, the truth is far more interesting, for it is inseparable from the history of the birth of our country.

In 1817, Congress decided that changes in the flag were necessary, as earlier two more states had been added, resulting in two more stripes and two more stars. The Flag Act of 1818 called for a permanent 13 stripes. States would be recognized by stars only.

In 1912, President Taft issued executive orders prescribing the exact configuration of the national flag, including the precise width of its stripes and the diameter of its stars. A federal law known as the Flag Code, prescribing flag etiquette, was endorsed in 1943.

President Woodrow Wilson presented a beautiful Flag Day message in 1917:

"This flag, which we honor and under which we serve, is the emblem of our unity, our power, our thought and purpose as a nation. It has no other character than that which we give it from generation to generation. The choices are ours. It floats in majestic silence above the hosts that execute those choices, whether in peace or in war. And yet, though silent, it speaks to us—speaks to us of the past, of the men and women who went before us, and of the records they wrote upon it.

"We celebrate the day of its birth; and from its birth until now it has witnessed a great history, has floated on high the symbol of great events, of a great plan of life worked out by a great people...."

Each year on June 14, Flag Day is celebrated by Presidential proclamation. "Old Glory," the affectionate nickname for our beloved flag, is attributed to a sea captain, William Driver of Salem, Mass., who proudly exclaimed as he viewed the flag floating from the masthead of his ship, "Old Glory! Old Glory!"

After the admission of Arizona as the 48th state in 1912, the banner remained the same until Alaska and Hawaii were admitted into the Union officially in 1960. We now proudly display 50 stars.

PROPER DEFINITIONS FOR THE FLAG

The Flag of the United States of America, referred to as the National Flag, is also known as the National Ensign, National Color and National Standard. The term "National Flag" is applicable regardless of size or manner of display, but the other terms have certain well-defined usages of long standing within the armed services.

"National Ensign" is used by the Navy in a general manner, although it actually indicates the National Flag flown by airplanes, ships and boats.

"National Color" pertains to flags carried by dismounted units of the landing force and is stubbier than the National Ensign.

"National Standard" is carried by mounted, mechanized and motorized units.

History of the Pledge

The original author of the Pledge was Francis Bellamy, who was born at Mount Morris, New York on May 18, 1855, and died on Aug. 28, 1931. He was ordained in 1879 at the Baptist church in Little Falls, New York. The pledge he wrote was first used at the dedication of the World's Fairgrounds in Chicago on Oct. 21, 1892, the 400th anniversary of the discovery of America, and has been recited from that day to this, with some changes, by adults and schoolchildren throughout our land.

The Rev. Bellamy's original wording was altered slightly by the First and Second National Flag Conferences in 1923 and 1924. His work was officially designated as the Pledge of Allegiance to the Flag in 1945. On June 14, 1954, Flag Day, President Dwight D. Eisenhower signed a law that added to the Pledge of Allegiance the compelling and meaningful words "under God."

• • •

"A thoughtful mind, when it sees a nation's flag, sees not the flag only, but the nation itself; and whatever may be its symbols, its insignia, he reads chiefly in the flag the government, the principles, the truths, the history which belongs to the nation that sets it forth."

—*Henry Ward Beecher*

The American Flag

Our flag is the symbol of the soul of America. Old Glory stands for the freedom of the individual to worship God has he chooses, to love whom he likes and work where he will.

Because the greatness of our nation lies in the unshaking devotion and dedication of the people to these principles, it is important that we continually bless our country by pledging our love and loyalty.

• • •

Dear Lord:

As the flags across our nation this day, compelling our thoughts to recall the blessings we have for living in these Unites States of America, we give thanks.

And though many different flags have flown in territories across our land and on our ships at sea, we now have one united flag with 50 beautiful stars to represent the people in all states living under the banner of liberty. And as is fitting, our flag has grown as our country has grown, from 13 stars to 50, to make "Old Glory" an ensign of glory.

On this proud day when we honor our flag and what it represents in valor and achievement by men who were inspired by a dauntless love for God and Country, we ask that we be given the strength and courage of our forefathers in handling our inheritance.

May we weld together as one nation, intent on being the hallmark of integrity and moral standards for the world. We pray for Thy abiding guidance as we strive to be the peacemakers for the oppressed of all races.

Help us leave a proud legacy for our children of a world free of war and fear and hunger.

May the Stars and Stripes born amid the strife of battle continue to be a banner of a nation pledged to liberty. Bless our planet and all its inhabitants. Amen.

THE FLAG SPEAKS

I stand for Freedom, broad and wide,
For Faith and Toleration;
I stand for Brotherhood and Love
Through every land and nation.
I am a symbol of the best;
A country free from strife,
Of Harmony and Peace and Trust
And all good things of life.
I stand for Progress, Growth and Health
In every occupation;
I stand for Happiness and joy,
I ripple from each steeple,
And say to you, "True dignity
Resides within the people!"
I stand for Equal Rights of all
Where flags shall be unfurled;
I stand for Freedom in all thought
Around the entire world!
I stand for Decency and law,
For guidance from above,
For Friendliness with every race,
For Harmony and Love!

—*Nona Keen Duffy*

FLAG DAY INVOCATION

On this day when we pause to honor our beloved flag, we feel the emotional tug to our hearts for the symbol it represents. Our country, our connection on common ground and a deep sense of loyalty stirs the inner reaches of our being. Our founders gave us a rich birthright, and we feel the obligation to perpetuate that proud heritage. We ask for Thy guidance in fulfilling that role.

May this day and this meeting be especially meaningful to our members, as we renew our patriotic spirit of oneness.

We give grateful thanks that we belong to this organization and that it gives us the opportunity to become bigger than a personal self and share in the higher pursuits of goodwill toward all mankind.

Grant us, we pray, the strength and courage to always do not what is pleasing but what is ethical and moral, so we can face our motives in the glaring light of noonday.

Bless the leaders of our country and give them the wisdom to make the right decisions in fulfilling their vows to uphold our constitution and keep faith with the people of this great United States of America.

May our beloved flag and country be under Thy infinite hand.

Help guide this troubled world to a state of peace and prosperity. Amen.

INDEPENDENCE DAY (July 4)

General Washington, when the Star-Spangled Banner was first flown by the Continental Army, is said to have described its symbolism as follows:

"We take the stars from heaven, the red from our mother country, separating it by the white stripes, thus showing that we have separated from her, and the white stripes shall go down to posterity representing liberty."

Thomas Jefferson wrote the Declaration of Independence that was approved by the Continental Congress on the hot evening of July 4, 1776. Nine colonies voted in favor of the resolution at that time. John Hancock, president of the Congress, signed the document to make it official, and so it is reported, "with a great flourish," he declared, "There, King George can read that without spectacles!"

These 56 patriots realized their great personal danger in this proceeding. "And for the support of this declaration, with a firm reliance on the protection of Divine Providence, we mutually pledge to each other our lives, our fortunes and our sacred honor." They thus signed.

At noon on July 8, 1776, the Declaration was read in Independence Square, and again that evening. Citizens hearing the document lit bonfires, and church bells pealed. The great bell, "Province Bell," rang out. Its name was later changed to "Liberty Bell," for its appropriate inscription: "Proclaim Liberty Throughout All the Land Unto All the Inhabitants Thereof." Independence Day, our most patriotic holiday, is celebrated with parades and festive observances in all states. The Philippine Islands also celebrate July 4 as their national day of independence. They chose this day to express appreciation for America honoring the promise of granting their independence.

WE THE PEOPLE
Our forefathers were wise and brave,
And left us a valuable heritage;
They founded a nation in Liberty,
Their motto being, "In God We Trust!"
Our Nation was built on a Spiritual base,
To love God with all our strength
And to love our neighbor as ourself!
If we live up to this wise admonition,
Our responsibility to history
Will be fulfilled in a glorious way;
Our nation will thrive and prosper
And we shall continue to enjoy our Republic;
We shall enjoy Freedom of Movement,
Freedom of Speech, Freedom of Spirit,
And so develop the health of our nation
And add to the happiness of all!

Let us resolve to preserve our freedom
And perpetuate our liberties!
Let us move forward in love and trust
Toward the noblest dream conceived by man!
Let us love God with all our heart,
And our neighbors as we love ourself!
Let us maintain our Ship of State,
Our country, "One Nation Under God."

—*Nona Keen Duffy*

THE AMERICAN'S CREED

I believe in the United States of America, as a government of the people, by the people, for the people; whose just powers are derived from the consent of the governed; a democracy in a republic; a sovereign nation of many sovereign states; a perfect union, one and inseparable; established upon those principles of freedom, equality, justice and humanity for which American patriots sacrificed their lives and fortunes.

I therefore believe it is my duty to my country to love it, to support its constitution, to obey its laws, to respect its flag, and to defend it against all enemies.

—*William Tyler Page*

(Adopted by Act of Congress April 6, 1918)

• • •

Dear God:

On this special day of celebration when we lift our spirits joyfully to sing in unison, "Happy Birthday, America," we give thanks for our great heritage, created by dauntless men of courage and moral character. May we take pride in our country as we discard the bonds of ruthless bigotry and harsh judgements of our neighbors in the world. Help us practice the faith of our forefathers. We earnestly pray that all men will one day know the joy of true liberty and the pursuit of happiness as their birthright. Bless us and all the peoples throughout every land. Amen.

• • •

Dear Father,

On this day of independence of our country, let us honor our forefathers who were the visionaries of their time, showing resourcefulness, self-determination and unity of spirit.

Help us keep those outstanding characteristics firmly in our minds as we celebrate our individual and national freedom.

For this devotion to loyalty to our country and to our Creator, we pay homage and pray that we ever keep the American dream alive in our hearts.

Thank You, God, for this meeting, and bless us as we ask that peace and harmony be established throughout the world. Let us further Thy work by holding hands with our brothers. Amen.

•••

MY COUNTRY

God grant that not only the love of liberty,
But a thorough knowledge of the rights of man
May pervade all nations of the earth,
So that a philosopher may set his foot
Anywhere on its surface and say "This is my country."

—*Benjamin Franklin*

•••

INDEPENDENCE DAY INVOCATION

Dear God:

As we celebrate the birth of our nation with noise and fireworks displays, we also proclaim thankfulness for our personal and national freedom. As Americans, our Independence Day is every day.

In observing this holiday, we also recongize our obligation to honor all people's religious independence. As our forefathers suffered the Revolutionary War to gain separation from mother country or fatherland, we know that war will not manifest peace or instill peace in the hearts of mankind.

O God, we know that prayer is powerful. Please revitalize our faith in prayer so that more and more people lend their prayers for peace into the cumulative race consciousness so that a transforming effect will encircle our globe. We are deeply grateful for this opportunity to meet together—rejoice together — celebrate and pray together. We demonstrate true independence when we put our faith in God for our inner and outer support.

Bless this membership and all the people of the world. We pray that the bells of freedom may ring in every land. Amen.

• • •

Teach us, O God, to ever appreciate our priceless heritage; to guard and preserve it through all trials and difficulties.

Grant that mankind may soon usher in the long-awaited millennium when Thy tabernacle of lasting peace shall be spread over all the inhabitants of the earth. Amen.

—Rabbi Sidney S. Guthman

190

VETERANS DAY

Veterans Day (formerly Armistice Day) was celebrated on Nov. 11 as the anniversary of the signing of the armistice ending World War I after four years of conflict.

In November, 1919, President Woodrow Wilson made the first Armistice Day proclamation, and the day was observed throughout the United States with veteran parades and patriotic services.

On Nov. 11, 1921, the casket of the Unknown Soldier was lowered into the tomb, with flags flying throughout the country at half mast. The inscription reads: "Here rests in honored glory an American Soldier known but to God."

But it was not until 1938 that Congress passed a bill that each Nov. 11 "shall be dedicated to the cause of world peace... hereafter celebrated and known as Armistice Day." Shortly before World War II, veterans groups pushed to change Nov. 11 to "Veterans Day" to honor all who had fought in American wars.

On May 24, 1954, the name was changed by an Act of Congress. President Eisenhower in his proclamation referred to the change to Veterans Day "in honor of the service men of all America's wars."

The most impressive ceremony is at the Tombs of the Unknowns at Arlington National Cemetery. In the 1960 exercises, a flaming torch was present from Antwerp, Belgium, and was accepted as "a symbol for the timeless effort for peace." This torch will continue to burn in Arlington in memory of our war dead.

NATIONALLY RECOGNIZED BIRTHDAYS AND COMMEMORATIVE DAYS

(Note: Invocations and prayers for religious holidays and family observances will not be found in this chapter, as these are personal or sacramental occasions often customized by traditional ceremonies. In deference to the individualized nature of these events, organizations usually suspend normal business sessions. Therefore, homilies for these specialized occasions have not been included. New Years Day and Thanksgiving are the exceptions, as organizations often hold a commemorative affair before, during or after the scheduled holiday.)

•••

NEW YEAR'S DAY (Jan. 1)
New Year's Day is the oldest and most celebrated holiday in the world. It is a legal holiday in the District of Columbia and all states.

Dear Members:
As we begin this January meeting with high hopes for a fresh start in every area of our lives, let us not forget to be thankful for the blessings in the past and put the experience gained into a useful direction. And may the resolutions we make serve to carry us into a brighter tomorrow, pointing the way to a star-studded future.

(See next page for Resolutions)

RESOLUTIONS

No one will ever get out of this world alive.

Resolve, therefore, in the year to come to maintain a sense of values.

Take care of yourself.

Good health is everyone's major source of wealth. Without it, happiness is almost impossible.

Resolve to be cheerful and helpful. People will repay you in kind.

Avoid angry, abrasive persons. They are generally vengeful.

Avoid zealots. They are generally humorless.

Resolve to listen more and to talk less. No one ever learns anything by talking.

Be chary of giving advice. Wise men don't need it, and fools won't heed it.

Resolve to be tender with the young, compassionate with the aged, sympathetic with the striving and tolerant of the weak and the wrong.

Sometime in life you will have been all of these.

Do not equate money with success. There are many successful money makers who are miserable failures as human beings.

What counts most about success is how a man achieves it.

Resolve to love next year someone you didn't love this year.

Love is the most enriching ingredient of life.

—*Walter Scott*

Dear Lord:

We ask that Thy love and guidance be with us throughout this coming year. We ask that our faith be renewed and we divert our attention away from what's wrong with the world, and look with hope and anticipation to a new global order of race consciousness wherein peace and brotherhood is the heart's desire of all peoples on earth. Amen.

INVOCATION FOR A NEW YEAR

Dear Lord:

As we greet this New Year full of joyful anticipation, let us also be grateful that we have learned from our yesterdays. We have learned not to dwell on the past, but accept it as a stepping stone into a brighter tomorrow. Now is the time we make our choices. As time requires the practice of patience, help us analyze our goals and commitments and resolve to put our priorities on matters dearest to our hearts.

Lord, we pray for wisdom in this direction. Allow us to set our sights higher than what could be expected, for if we aim only at the target, we will never hit the bull's-eye. We need to stretch ourselves to achieve and grow in strength of character. May Thy gems of inspiration light our path for the ensuing year.

And as we proceed, please help us remember to keep the joyful tune of "Good Tidings" echoing in our heads and heart. Grant that all our endeavors be of service to our fellowman and acceptable in Thy sight.

We pray the dove of peace will encircle this planet, and the wings of Almighty Love will shelter all mankind. Amen.

MARTIN LUTHER KING JR. DAY

Martin Luther King Jr. was a black civil rights leader, a minister and recipient of the Nobel Peace Prize in 1964. On Nov. 2, 1983, a law was signed to make Martin Luther King Jr.'s birthday a legal public holiday. The law sets the third Monday in January for the observance. The first observance was Jan. 20, 1986.

"Let brotherly love continue. Be not forgetful to entertain strangers: for thereby some have entertained angels unawares." *(Hebrews 13:1-2)*

•••

Dear Lord:

Let our compassion soar for those who are imprisoned in either their own minds or are in physical abuse of tyrants.

Help us seek ways to free the downtrodden in all walks of life and in any land that people cry for the joys of freedom.

We ask God in His glory to set free the brilliance of a sunrise to the spirit of the needy. When the air is pure and the breath is in tune with the rhythm of the seas, we can shout with joy and thanksgiving. And let us sing the immortal words of the great emancipator, the Rev. Martin Luther King, "Free at last, free at last. Thank God Almighty, I'm free at last."

•••

Dear Lord:

When we live in harmony with our brother, we see not only the outward manifestation, but the inner light that is the connection to God. By refusing to pass judgement on others, we refuel our lamps of kindness and earn our own personal self-respect.

We become winners in this role of life when we fail to look upon anyone as above or below us and see only into the heart and soul, the essence of God.

We add a candle to the growth of humanity, and we allow that light to burn brightly, protecting it from the wind or rains.

The storms will pass when we are dedicated to the higher ideals of a spiritual nature.

Dear God, we ask Thy blessings and guidance for the peacemakers. May their actions always stem from universal love and serve as beacons to a society crying for enlightenment. Let us entertain strangers and find angels. Amen.

• • •

VALENTINE'S DAY (Feb. 14)

The origin of St. Valentine's Day is clothed in mystery: what is legend, and what is truth? According to the Acta Sanctorum, there were actually eight men with the name, Valentine, seven of whose feast days were on Feb. 14.

One version holds that St. Valentine was put into prison for helping some Christians and while there cured a jailor's daughter of blindness, and as a consequence was beheaded Feb. 14, 269 A.D. In 496 Pope Gelasius set aside the date of his death to honor him. Another legend says that Valentine fell in love with the jailor's daughter and wrote letters to her, signing them "from your Valentine."

Whatever the facts are in its history, Valentine's Day has

become a day to openly express love and affection in a pragmatic way. Shakespeare and poets have written verses to commemorate and perpetuate the amorous theme. In England, the holiday has been observed for centuries. It is reported that in colonial times American merchants imported valentines from England.

Valentine's Day, like St. Patrick's Day, is not a legal holiday and not American in origin, but it has a definite place in the hearts of Americans for the message it conveys.

● ● ●

Let us remember this Valentine's Day, what the wise St. Augustine said, "Love and do what you like," so little does mere surface matter count.

Dear Lord:

The hearts and flowers displayed here today remind us that this day is set aside to express love openly, and it does not just belong to lovers. It is our unique time to look deeply into the realities of life from our love or soul nature.

We ask that our compassion be reinforced, and we surrender all false judgements of our fellowman. Help us love one another unreserved and exhibit those feelings in kind actions.

May we see ourselves and others as ambassadors to Your divine plan of universal love enfolding our planet Earth. We ask Thy guidance to reach that place where we know no saint or sinner, no freeman or bondsman, only each person as heir to Thy kingdom.

Let us mentally join hands with our brothers and sisters as we march forward in the unfoldment of our higher spiritual qualities. Give us, we pray, the vision to see our creative purpose and the will, strength and courage to bring it to fruition. We ask Thy loving Grace be with all our members and with the leaders of our country. And may their actions be based on love for all mankind. We give thanks for our multitudinous blessings. Amen.

ABRAHAM LINCOLN'S BIRTHDAY

The first formal celebration of Abraham Lincoln's birthday was given by President Andrew Johnson on Feb. 12, 1866. Although many states today celebrate the date as a legal holiday, the District of Columbia and other states do not. It is not a holiday for federal employees and was never proclaimed by Congressional action.

•••

Far better it is to dare mighty things, to win glorious triumphs, even though checked by failure, than to take rank with those poor spirits who neither enjoy much or suffer much, because they live in the gray twilight that knows neither victory nor defeat.

—Theodore Roosevelt

•••

Dear Lord:

Let us not rest blithely on the laurels of our reformed programs of the past when there is further progress to be made. May we hold out our hand in support to those who seem weighted down by race, creed or social discriminations. As we take our stand for the constitutional rights of others we add our weight to the scale of justice. Prejudice of any type is demeaning to America.

We ask God's grace in giving us the wisdom to take measures to alleviate the "gray twilight" from those lives who know neither victory or defeat.

By lifting our fellowman in stature, we add a link to the

chain of world consciousness that will one day release all people from fear and their dreams of peace and freedom from tyranny will become reality.

We ask that You continue to bless this nation and give us strength to beat the drum and blow the bugle of triumph so loudly that all humanity will be liberated from bias, and that joy, love, peace and brotherhood will reign on Earth. Amen.

• • •

GEORGE WASHINGTON'S BIRTHDAY

As it was a custom in colonial times to observe the British king's birthday each year; following the American Revolution many celebrations were given to honor General Washington, the "illustrious Commander-in-Chief." Although for many years all states and the District of Columbia celebrated Feb. 22 as a legal holiday in honor of our first President's birthday, the Monday holiday law, beginning in 1971, moved the date to the third Monday in February.

The holiday was renamed Presidents' Day to celebrate the birthdays of both Washington and Lincoln. Many regard this a day to recognize all former U.S. presidents, which loses the special significance of the observance. This date is ratified in most states as a legal holiday.

• • •

"It is impossible to govern the world without God. He must be worse than an infidel that lacks faith, and more than wicked that has not gratitude enough to acknowledge his obligation."

—*George Washington*

• • •

Dear Father:

Grant us the strength and courage to uphold the high principles of our forefathers. Help each do his/her part in fostering devotion to the United States through unwavering loyalty. Bless this meeting, and may each member take home an idea or inspiration that will help them rise to their full potential that Thou has created them for.

Bless and grant peace and prosperity to all the people of the world. And we pray that all humankind be released from the fear of fear. Amen.

• • •

Let us listen to the words of our first President:

"Without a humble imitation of the divine Author of our blessed religion, we can never hope to be a happy nation."

—*George Washington*

• • •

Dear God:

As we deliberate on the significance of this special day and month in which we honor the birthdays of great leaders and the makers of our history as a nation, we ask Thee to imbue us with the fervent spirit of our forefathers to march courageously forward to face all the barriers of this age and time that deter us from being the hallmark Republic envisioned by our founders. We pray for guidance and wisdom in these efforts.

It is not our heritage to settle for mediocrity in the union of world nations. Help us rekindle our patriotic spirit and renew our dedication to create a national consciousness of united brotherhood — one for all and all for one.

May our faith in Thy divine plan for this great nation echo loudly in our hearts and in the hearts of today's leaders. May they be blessed with wisdom, courage and integrity to keep our country on the path to fulfill the Great American Dream for us and our heirs.

We offer a special prayer that peace be established throughout our world. Amen.

●●●

ST. PATRICK'S DAY (March 17)

St. Patrick's Day is not a legal holiday for Americans, but millions of our countrymen turn "Irish" on this day, the date that honors the death of Patrick, Ireland's patron saint. St. Patrick, according to Roman Catholic authorities, was born in 387 A.D., not in Ireland, but at Kilpatrick, near Dumbarton, Scotland.

Clubs and organizations meeting before, on or shortly after this day use shamrocks and green decorations for the occasion. Truly, the legends have captured the hearts of Americans and that of other countries. As a result, St. Patrick's Day is a definite part of our culture.

A wee bit of background...

St. Patrick, a fervent missionary bishop who preached and baptized thousands of converts during his 40 years of "apostolic zeal" in Ireland, also established churches, schools and consecrated a few colleges. There are many legends surrounding his life and works, so it is difficult to distinguish between truth, miracles and mystery. Because the Irish are naturally adventurous, they emigrated to many parts of the globe. As a

201

result, St. Patrick's Day is celebrated world-wide. Irish societies were founded as early as 1737. The first celebration in honor of this saint is said to have taken place in Boston, and the idea spread rapidly to other cities, with groups and societies sponsoring the affair. General George Washington had many Irishmen in his army. Today, New York City is noted for its lavish St. Patrick's Day parade.

The catchy Irish folk melodies and Irish jigs, along with feasting, drinking and frolicking for the sake of St. Patrick, has captured the affection of millions of Americans, who proudly wear green and display shamrocks on March 17.

This display of mutual merry-making demonstrates that the lives of all races of the world are deeply entwined and the prospect for an eventual world peace and global brotherhood is not the idle wish of a dreamer. If, from St. Patrick's death, March 17, 493, the memory of St. Patrick can be kept alive today, in the hearts of men, nothing is impossible.

"What man dares to dream, he can achieve."

•••

LAW DAY

Celebrated on May 1, Law Day is to many countries what our Labor Day in September is to us — a tribute paid to the loyal workers and their interests. The May Day celebrated by school children with flowers and dancing around maypoles, is a custom originating in Great Britain.

In 1961, President John F. Kennedy issued a proclamation asking all Americans to display the Stars and Stripes on Law Day and to observe the date "with suitable ceremonies."

Law Day is "a day set aside for Americans to rededicate themselves to the principle of individual freedom under law."

Although this holiday is not celebrated by the majority of clubs and associations, it is being included in this chapter for recognition of its importance in our daily lives—to give respect and honor to those who are dedicated to those tenets of upholding the law for protection and freedom of individual rights.

• • •

Dear God:

On these patriotic occasions, we are reminded of our role in the future of our country. Our founding fathers gave us a legacy to uphold the honorable principles of truth, dignity for the individual and integrity in all dealings with the supreme purpose of "justice for all."

May we stay ever steadfast to the meritorious morals of the past. The blood, sweat and tears that were shed to conquer and subdue this great land must not be washed from our minds. Help us keep the spirit of unity ever evolving to greater heights through pride in a system that guarantees and protects the individual's right to freedom under law and order.

We ask a rededication of love and loyalty to our country be established in our hearts and the minds and hearts of all Americans across this great land. And may we all become worthy world citizens by loving thoughts, words, actions and deeds.

May Thy blessings and Grace go with all those who are in command of keeping the peace and distributing justice. Give them, we pray, the infinite wisdom to fulfill these duties. We know, Thy grace is our sufficiency.

"And God is able to make all grace abound toward you; that ye, always having all sufficiency in all things, may abound to every good work." (II Corinthians 9:8 KJV) Amen.

• • •

LABOR DAY

At a meeting in May, 1882, Peter J. McGuire, president of the United Brotherhood of Carpenters and Joiners of America proposed to the New York Central Labor Union that a "Labor Day" be noted on the first Monday in September. He wanted to observe a festive day, during which a parade through the streets of the city would permit public tribute to American industry.

A Salute to Labor Day

This Labor Day, it is fitting that we take this holiday break between the end of summer and beginning of strenuous fall activities to pay tribute to the achievements of our American industrial system and the organizations who have paved the way to dignify the labor scene and give it a status of recognition and pride.

The churches and free labor are both striving for the end of poverty in the world and peace among nations.

In this typically American holiday, we are proud to glorify work, our organizations, and be grateful to our Creator for making today's workplace a position of honor and dignity, unlike the status of disrespect in the past. We give grateful recognition to the founders of the Labor Day movement. They deserve our praise for initiating a day to recognize the achievements and pay deserved respects to the millions of workers who have made our country great.

Let us remember to give thanks to God for the Infinite treasure of energy and enthusiasm. With a fervent spirit, we heed the words, "and let us not be weary in well doing, for in due season we shall reap, if we faint not." (Galatians 6:9)

●●●

COLUMBUS DAY (Oct. 12)

We can all take a lesson from that dauntless explorer, Columbus, the Italian Admiral who was about to submit to his men's demands to turn back and give up the expedition. Then, the joyful shouts from the lookout on the Pinta pierced through the gloom: "Tierra! Tierra!"

His son, Ferdinand Columbus, described that memorable day: "After all had rendered thanks unto our Lord, kneeling on the ground and kissing it with tears of joy for his great favor to them, the Admiral rose and gave this island the name San Salvador. Then, in the presence of the many natives assembled there, he took possession of it in the name of the Catholic Sovereigns with appropriate ceremony and words."

Columbus Day is celebrated in all Pan-American lands, as an anniversary of the discovery of America. This is a very patriotic holiday and also a religious occasion. We can well give thanks to our divine creator for the care and guidance which has directed our history and American destiny.

Our country has been abundantly blessed. As we honor Columbus as a pioneer explorer, who had the vision and the faith in God to pursue that vision against overwhelming odds, we learn the lesson that courage, faith and persistence will prevail.

• • •

It is reported that the first celebration of the discovery of America occurred in New York City on Oct. 12, 1792, when the order of Columbia (or St. Tammany) held a dinner in honor of Columbus.

Benjamin Harrison, president of the United States made a proclamation appointing Friday, Oct. 12, 1892, the 400th anniversary of the discovery of America, as a general holiday for the people of the United States.

It wasn't until Sept. 1934 that President Franklin D. Roosevelt issued a proclamation asking all 48 states to observe Oct 12 as a national holiday.

However, it was not until the Monday Holiday Law in 1970 that Columbus Day was recognized nationwide.

Today, millions of Americans enjoy the second Monday in October as a three-day holiday, with little regard to the significance.

Yet, the words of Joaquin Miller about Columbus should echo through this land: *"He gained a world; he gave that world its grandest lesson: "On! Sail on!"*

And another American has stated that Christopher Columbus was the greatest educator that ever lived, for he emancipated humanity from the narrowness of its ignorance... and taught the lesson that human destiny, like divine mercy, arches over the whole world.

• • •

THANKSGIVING (Fourth Thursday in November)

A legal holiday in all states, the District of Columbia, the Canal Zone, Guam, Puerto Rico and the Virgin Islands.

This distinctly American holiday is a legacy of the pilgrims. After anxious times waiting for the yield of their crops for survival, the Gov. William Bradford of the Colony declared "between the hours of 9 and 12 in the day time, on Thursday, November ye 29th of the year of our lord one thousand six hundred and twenty-three, and the third year since ye Pilgrims landed on Ye Pilgrim Rock, there to listen to ye pastor, and render thanksgiving to ye Almighty God for all His blessings."

It is reported that this was the second Thanksgiving , but the one in 1621, historians do not give any reference to a feast of religious nature. There is no evidence that a day of "thanks" was an annual observance.

President George Washington was the first President to make a Thanksgiving Day proclamation Oct. 3, 1789. He proclaimed: "It is the duty of nations to acknowledge the providence of Almighty God, to obey His will, to be grateful for his benefits, and humbly to implore His protection and favor..."

Three years after the War of 1812, President Madison proclaimed a special Thanksgiving for peace. After that some of the states held their own observances, but it was not until the victory at Gettysburg that President Lincoln issued a proclamation naming the last Thursday in November as the date in 1863. Later presidents followed his example.

● ● ●

Dear Lord:

Unlike those brave pilgrims who founded a Colony in Plymouth Rock and prayed for rain and a bountiful harvest of their small plot of crops, we meet centuries later, reaping a magnitude of abundance in all areas of life, that could not have been envisioned by the greatest dreamer of that period. Truly from small acorns the giant oak trees grow.

When we look back into history and marvel at the heroes of the past, we must also acknowledge the heroes of the present who have made this amazing progress possible. We cannot, like our forefathers, help but recognize the hand of Divine Providence in bringing us to this point in time. We humbly thank you, God.

With advancement and knowledge comes the responsibility to stretch ever higher for spiritual discernment, "Man does not live on bread alone... but by every word that proceedeth out of the mouth of God."

We ask that Thy grace be with us in granting us the wisdom in becoming caretakers of our world and the afflicted and needy upon this planet. Unlike Columbus, who could sail out to seek a new world, we must share this with all humankind. Teach us to be benefactors and beacons of light, setting examples for generations to come who will have from our efforts only a path of peace to tread.

We are grateful for the legacy of the past. Help us, we pray, to leave a legacy to the future, so that every American will be proud to say, "I did my part in the divine destiny of my country." Amen.

FOREFATHER'S DAY
Look back 300 years and more;
A group upon a rock-bound shore,
Borne by the Mayflower o'er the sea,
Pledged hearts and lives to liberty.

They were the few we hail with pride,
Singing; "Land where our fathers died."
Daring to die that this might be
Forever: "Land of the noble free."

At Plymouth Rock they could not know
How far their shadows then would go.
That freedom (as today we sing)
From every mountainside should ring.

"Our Fathers' God to Thee" I pray
That we, devoted as were they,
Who sing "Long may our land be bright"
Shall cherish "Freedom's holy light.
                              —*Edgar A. Guest*

Invocations for Specialized Groups

COMMUNITY SERVICE AWARDS
Dear Father:

We give thanks for Thy invisible presence on our meeting, which is held to honor those members who have dedicated their services to aid the less fortunate of our human race. We take exceeding pride in their efforts to uplift the spirits and living conditions of their charges. They have indeed proved the words of Alexander Graham Bell: "When one door closes, another opens."

We ask a special blessing be bestowed on these members who have selflessly donated their time and energies to give new hope and restore faith of the down-trodden. By their actions, they have perhaps unknowingly added an extra dimension to all of us. May they wear their halos with the proud bearing of a soldier of mercy.

Dear God, as we rejoice on this special occasion, we request Thy guidance and blessing on the membership and this meeting.

We ask that the love displayed here be transmitted to all peoples in every part of our world, and the "peace that passeth all understanding" will soon reign on earth. Amen.

• • •

PERSONAL RECOGNITION

Dear God:

We meet today in celebration to honor these members for their outstanding achievements.

Our hearts are swelled with mutual pride in the high standard they set for themselves in excellence. And we are grateful that their personal success is also a reflection of tribute to our organization and its distinguished purposes.

We rejoice in the awards they so nobly earned.

And God, let us not forget that the incentive for accomplishment is born from within and is sparked by Thy eternal love, for which we give our unstinting "thanks."

May Thy benevolent blessings be with these members, their families and our absent members.

Grant, we pray, the cessation of conflict between individuals, races and nations, so peace and goodwill toward all men will come to pass. Amen.

● ● ●

SLATE OF NEW OFFICERS

Dear God:

We ask Thy divine blessing upon this meeting. Help us to uphold the principles and noble intents of our founders as we chart our course for this New Year. Please give our officers the enthusiasm and wisdom to fulfill their appointed duties. And in appreciation of their loyal efforts, may the membership always support them.

May we cultivate a sincere and loving heart, a faith that never falters and a deep desire to aid our fellowman. Let us not be only hearers of kind acts, but also doers of good works.

We humbly pray for the earnest good will to see all tasks through to completion as we put forth the hand of brotherhood to all in need.

Dear God, thank you for the multitude of blessings You have bestowed on each of us. Please be with our absent members and lighten those who carry heavy burdens.

We pray that Thy abiding peace be established in this troubled world, and that love and understanding fill the hearts of all men and women on earth.

Let us remember Thy words: "With God, all things are possible." (Matthew 19:26) Amen.

• • •

INVOCATIONS FOR SERVICE ORGANIZATIONS
Dear Lord:
We humbly ask that Thy transcendent presence be with us as we open this meeting today.

Our grateful thanks is extended for this opportunity to put forth joint efforts in becoming channels for good to function and prosper — helping others regain their self respect.

Help us lay the foundation of success rather than failure in individual lives. May we supplant fear with faith and align it with love.

We know that in the deep tapestry of life is woven golden threads of hope for the down-hearted. As we offer our services to weave this beneficial element into the lives of others, our lives become richer. Please give us the wisdom and insight to do justice to our appointed tasks.

We pray we can be instruments in helping promote peace and goodwill amongst our community and the nations of the world. Please bless all our endeavors. Amen.

• • •

ELECTION TIME

Dear God:

As we meet today, with the membership of this great organization, we ask that we practice tolerance and understanding during this period of decision on the leadership of our (country/organization).

Our purpose is not to take sides on any political issue. We faithfully follow that principle in the business of club operation during our meetings.

Let our hearts and minds be filled with pride in the contribution our country has made to the world by displaying the benefits of freedom.

Help us to remember that we are 100 percent Americans, no matter where we or our ancestors were born. The United States is our homeland and haven for liberty. We ask Thy blessing on every person from "sea to shining sea."

We give grateful thanks for guidance in all our affairs — personal, social and business. May love, harmony, cooperation and mutual assistance be the foundation for all our actions.

Please be with our absent members.

We join together in our united prayer for peace to be established throughout the world. Amen.

• • •

A PRAYER FOR TIMES OF INTERNAL CONFLICT
Dear God:

In this day of inner and outer turbulence, we come to Thee with open hearts. Help us view the dirt of disorder in its proper perspective as a murky scene which has come to pass. May we raise our sights to the cloudless sky above.

Help us become impersonal to personal attacks of criticism and hostility, so we do not anger and give our adversary the edge. O Lord, keep us from pettiness.

We ask Thy guidance in our efforts to solve our dilemma. Let us heed Thy words, "Love your neighbor as yourself.

Our humble prayer is to receive Thy eternal love and let it pass through us to the outermost limits of our world. Bless this membership as we hold our cup of kindness out to those in need.

Grant peace and understanding to us and to all the peoples sharing space on our beautiful planet Earth. Amen.

• • •

God is my strength and power and he maketh my way perfect. (II Samuel 22:33)

Dear Father, we accept Thy strength, Thy power and the perfect way for each of these beloved members and their families. Amen.

• • •

BUSINESS MEETING

Dear Father:

We know for a business to prosper and survive, service must remain uppermost in the minds of the top executives and all those involved in the operation.

Harmony is also a vital component to success, and only by each person fulfilling their particular station with expertise and efficiency will progress become the motto in the organization.

Queen Christina said, "It is necessary to try to surpass one's self always; this occupation ought to last as long as life."

We ask God to give us the incentive and to hold fast to this honorable industry of constant improvement of self and service. Expand our knowledge to accept whatever changes may be called for to produce a better product.

May our relationships with one another be based on mutual trust, sincerity of motive and a deep-seated bonding of love and respect. With these high principles firmly implanted in our minds and hearts, we will be invincible in the face of all obstacles on our chosen path of excellence.

We ask Thy blessings in all our undertakings.

May peace, love and understanding enter the hearts of all mankind. Amen.

•••

SALES MEETING

Dear Lord:

Bless our meeting and the camaraderie it brings. May each member be aware that he must sell himself before he can sell to buyers. To become a master salesman, we must think kindly of ourselves, and we do this by knowing that we are one with the Infinite and important to the universal plan of life. Although we know that God does not judge, we tend to judge ourselves, and often too harshly.

Help each of us be more kind and gentle with ourselves and be open and receptive to divine guidance to reach our full potential. May we learn to live without inner conflict and accept harmony as our spiritual inheritance.

May we hold steadfast to the high principles of our organization, so our goals will never be out of reach.

We ask that our prayers go out to help lighten the hearts of all people around the world, and grant peace to all nations. Amen.

•••

FOR ENVIRONMENTALIST GROUPS

and those organizations devoted to peace and the welfare of our planet

Robert Muller, author of "New Genesis," wrote a dedication in his book worthy of reading at meetings, to help infuse the membership with a clarion call to action.

Here are some excerpts:

"I dedicate this book to the innumerable good people of this planet who want to live in peace, friendship, freedom and justice, and to enoy the miracle of life under the generous rays of our sun and the good guidance of the God of the universe.

"It is dedicated to all peacemakers who try to heal the antiquated quarrels, divisions and insanity of those who refuse to recognize the oneness of our planetary home and of the human family.

"It is dedicated to the United Nations, the first universal organization on this planet, from which I have learned so much.

"May the kind divine providence help us start a new history and new human relationships as we approach the bimillenium.

"Let us all coaelesce with all our strength, mind, heart and soul around a New Genesis, a true global, God-abiding political, moral and spiritual renaissance to make this planet at long last what it was always meant to be: the Planet of God."

—*Robert Muller, author New Genesis*
Chancellor, University for Peace, Costa Rica
Former Assistant Secretary-General, United Nations
(Reproduced with permission of World Happiness and Cooperation, PO Box 1153, Anacortes, WA 98221.)

Author's Note: See the Appendix for more resources on this subject.

CHAPTER 11
Memorial Services

• Prayers and Inspirations for Organizations and Private Ceremonies

CHAPTER 11
Memorial Services

Mark Twain said, "Let us endeavor so to live that, when we come to die, even the undertaker will be sorry."

Some organizations have rites they perform at their memorial services. The presiding officer may put on that part of the ceremony and then call on the chaplain for the prayer. Or, it may be the duty of the chaplain to conduct the whole observance.

Throughout history, all cultures have had ceremonies to symbolize rites of passage from one stage in life to another — birth, puberty, marriage and death, to name a few.

Candles are symbolic in nearly all religious ceremonies and represent consummation of the old past patterns of life — ideas — beliefs to make way for a new and deeper spiritual experience. Ribbons and colors often are used to symbolize qualities of the spirit, or initiation into a new state of consciousness. Flowers and wreaths may also be used in a ceremony to honor the memory of past members.

THE SIGNIFICANCE OF CANDLES

The light of the candle has three aspects: the invisible essence of the flame, the light, and the heat. Close to the wick is a faint blue glow. Around this is a ring of golden light, and further out there is a light reddish flame, which gives off more or less smoke.

To some religious orders, the flame represents the Trinity of God. Others draw parallels to the flame of life in man. The blue flame represents the spirit; the yellow, the life and light of mind; and the reddish glow with heat, the fire of sex, desire and

221

personal drive, which distinguishes man from any other creature. The flame of the candle is like man's soul, ever stretching to empyrean heights.

•••

COMMEMORATIONS

When a member or relative of a member suffers a loss or tragedy, it is considerate and appropriate for the chaplain to entertain a moment of silence before delivering the invocation.

You may wish to preface it with a statement of the circumstances. Say:

"Let us observe a moment of silence to remember our dear member,_____. Our heartfelt condolence is extended to his family in their bereavement. May God give comfort to these loved ones and to us in our loss." (Silence follows.)

After the commemoration, the Chaplain may go directly into the invocation. On these occasions, choosing an invocation of shorter length is advisable, so your presentation does not intrude on the timing of the meeting.

Sometimes, an appropriate Bible verse is quoted. For example:

"Fear not, for I have redeemed you; I have called you by name. You are mine. (Isaiah 43:1)

A quotation may also be read after the silence:

"Go forth in your longing to the fields, and sit by the lilies, and you shall hear them humming in the sun. They weave not cloth for raiment, nor do they raise wood or stone for shelter, yet they sing. He who works in the night fulfills their needs, and the dew of His grace is upon their petals. And are not you also His care, who never wearies nor rests?"

—Kahlil Gibran

The chaplain may then say "Let us pray."

The "sympathy" section of your local card store has many comforting and appropriate messages to choose from. Refer to the appendix for further sources.

●●●

CONVENTION MEMORIALS

Because of the time lapse between conventions, most organizations schedule a memorial service in their program to commemorate past members.

Each association's requirements are unique, but the following suggestions may help kindle the creative energies of the person assigned to perform the memorial service. One's own inner heart wisdom will always be the best source.

Introductions:

This is the time we pay homage to our members who have departed from our ranks.

We cherish the memory of their presence and the contribution they made to our organization and to our personal lives. The light and love of their presence will live long in our hearts. We are grateful that during their pilgrimage on earth they chose to bless us by becoming united with us.

Unstintingly, we offer our affection and compassion to the families of these members and extend our hands and hearts to them for support.

We pray the Lord will give them the same comforting, loving arms to welcome them into their new home as were given when they entered into this life.

To our membership we say that Easter, a springtime celebration of renewal and rebirth, is not only a one-day event. Every day repeats the glories of awakening to a new day, a new hour, a new moment.

As we take this time in thoughtful contemplation of the meaning of life and the resurrection of the spirit, we give thanks that our faith is firm in the promise of life everlasting.

We here today acknowledge this occasion as an Easter of springtime and transformation for our loved ones and ourselves. We are not downcast, but uplifted with prayers of praise and thanksgiving for the understanding that we all are nurtured in the soil of darkness and tenderly pushed toward the sunlight. With steadfast faith, we grow and mature into a beautiful blossom with the color, the fragrance and beauty one rose gives to the world.

Let us pray:

Dear God:

Despite moments of darkness, when we do not see the light that is hidden behind the dark clouds, we can take comfort in Thy words: "Weeping may tarry for the night, but joy comes with the morning." (Psalms 30:5)

We give grateful thanks for Thy everpresent love and protection. Guide us, we pray, to our ultimate good, that we may serve Thee and our fellow man more fully.

We accept Thy promise of joy in the morning and will endeavor to spread it to others as a birthright of our blessing for being a missionary on Thy planet Earth. Amen.

●●●

Or:

Dear friends and members, we take this moment to pay homage to our deceased members who have passed from our sight, but not from our hearts.

Each of us knows what lasting memory we hold of the difference they made to our organization and to our lives.

We honor them and give grateful thanks that we were brought together to enrich our lives and benefit our fellow man.

Shall we pray:

Dear God:

We know full well that the concept of death has an abstract meaning for most of us. We desire with all our hearts to believe that this hidden journey is one of transformation to a higher realm of being, that supernal eternity is granted to our loved ones and will be the path we, too, will tread when we have finished our pilgrimage on this Earth.

Give us the trust and security of Thy infinite love, so that as we walk in the light of the wonders of life we may not tremble with fear of the unknown.

We have been told to seek the heart of life, to unlock the mystery of death. Let us remember the springtime, with its rebirth of new leaves, the glad songs of birds and the fresh winds penetrating our soul.

If life and death are one harmonious flow of the currents of life, like the tides of the oceans, let us bounce on the foam of the wave.

Let us relish the splendor of today and dream of the majesty of tomorrow, more joy-filled than we can envision. May our departed discover ways of riding in the clouds and float with softness through the heavens of all eternity.

Bless us and those who are now on the journey to other mansions. We seek God with our hearts. Only when we sit in the serenity of silence is the veil to the mystery of life and death parted for a faint peek.

Let us have a moment of silence to remember our brothers and sisters. We ask God's speed for the full illumination of their eternal soul. (Silence follows.) Amen.

"Behold, now is the acceptable time; behold, now is the day of salvation." (II Corinthians 6:2)

• • •

The following selections of prose may be used as the introduction into the memorial service, followed by your personalized prayer, or vice versa.

ETERNAL VISION
They know me not, who think that I am
    only flesh and blood...
    a transient dweller on this fragile spaceship earth
    that gave me human birth
For I am spirit
    eternal, indestructible, not confined to space or time
    and when my sojourn here is through
    my roles fulfilled, my assignments done
    I will lay aside this spacesuit called my body
    and move on to other mansions, roles, assignments
    in our father's house of eternal life.
So dry your tears
    weep not overmuch for me — or for yourself
    set me free, in the love that holds us all
    and makes us one eternally!
Our paths will cross again
    our minds and hearts will touch
    our souls will shout with joy and laughter
    as we recall the lives we've lived
    the worlds we've seen, the ways we've trod
    to find ourselves — at last —
        in God.

—*J. Sig Paulson*

THE EVERLASTING LIGHT

Those we love must someday pass
   beyond our present sight...
      must leave us
and the world we know
   without their
      radiant light.
   But we know
      that like a candle
   their lovely light
      will shine
   to brighten up
      another place
more perfect... more divine.
      And in the realm of Heaven
where they shine
   so warm and bright,
our loved ones live forevermore
   in God's eternal light.

—Unknown

• • •

227

I cannot say and I will not say
    That he is dead. He is just away!
With a cheery smile and a wave of the hand
    He has wandered into an unknown land,
And left us dreaming how very fair
    It needs must be, since he lingers there,
And you — O you, who the wildest years
    For the old-time step and the glad return —
Think of him faring on, as dear
    In the love of there as the love of here;
Think of him still as the same, I say;
    He is not dead — he is just away!

                      —*James Whitcomb Riley*

● ● ●

A PRAYER OF ST. FRANCIS OF ASSISI

Lord, make me an instrument of your peace.
Where there is hatred, let me sow love.
Where there is injury, pardon.
Where there is doubt, faith.
Where there is despair, hope.
Where there is darkness, light,
    and where there is sadness, joy.
O Divine Master, grant that I may
    not so much seek to be consoled
    as to console;
To be understood as to understand;
To be loved, as to love;
For it is in giving that we receive
It is in pardoning that we are pardoned;
And it is in dying that we are born to eternal life.

● ● ●

WHAT IS LIFE?

...If you can tell me what is death, then I will tell you what is life.

In a field, I have watched an acorn, a thing so still and seemingly useless. And in the spring I have seen that acorn take roots and rise, the beginning of an oak tree, toward the sun.

Surely you would deem this a miracle, yet that miracle is wrought a thousand thousand times in the drowsiness of every autumn and the passion of every spring.

Why shall it not be wrought in the heart of man? Shall not the seasons meet in the hand or upon the lips of a Man Anointed?

If our God has given to earth the art to nestle seed whilst the seed is seemingly dead, why shall He not give to the heart of man to breathe life into another heart, even a heart seemingly dead?

—Kahlil Gibran
Reprinted from
<u>*The Prophet*</u> *(c) 1923 Alfred A. Knopf, publisher*

● ● ●

THE ANGEL OF PATIENCE

To weary hearts, to mourning homes,
God's meekest Angel gently comes;
No power has he to banish pain
Or give us back our lost again;
And yet in tenderest love our dear
And heavenly Father sends him here.

There's quiet in that Angel's glance,
There's rest in his still countenance!
He mocks no grief with idle cheer,
Nor wounds with words the mourner's ear;
But ills and woes he may not cure
He kindly trains us to endure.

Angel of Patience, sent to calm
Our feverish brows with cooling palm;
To lay the storms of hope and fear,
And reconcile life's smile and tear;
The throbs of wounded pride to still,
And make our own our Father's will!

O thou who mournest on thy way,
With longings for the close of day;
He walks with thee, that Angel kind,
And gently whispers, "Be resigned;
Bear up, bear up, the end shall tell
The dear Lord ordereth all things well!"

—*John G. Whittier*

• • •

LIFE IS EVERLASTING

And his heart was moved with compassion, and he said:

"Life is older than all things living; even as beauty was winged ere the beautiful was born on earth, and even as truth was truth ere it was uttered.

"Life sings in our silences, and dreams in our slumber. Even when we are beaten and low, Life is enthroned and high. And when we weep, Life smiles upon the day, and is free even when we drag our chains."

—*Kahlil Gibran*

• • •

FOOD FOR THOUGHT

Many people seem to feel that science has somehow made "religious ideas" untimely or old-fashioned. But I think science has a real surprise for the skeptics. Science, for instance, tells us that nothing in nature, not even the tiniest particle, can disappear without a trace. Nature does not know extinction. All it knows is transformation.

Now, if God applies this fundamental principle to the most minute and insignificant parts of His universe, doesn't it make sense to assume that He applies it also to the human soul? I think it does. And everything science has taught me — and continues to teach me — strengthens my belief in the continuity of our spiritual existence after death. Nothing disappears without a trace.

—*Dr. Wernher von Braun*

• • •

When one door closes,
Another door opens —
But we often look so long
And so regretfully
Upon the closed door
That we do not see the ones
Which open for us.

—Alexander Graham Bell

• • •

SCRIPTURE VERSES

"Surely goodness and mercy shall follow me all the days of my life, and I will dwell in the house of the Lord forever." (Psalms 23:6)

• • •

"A new heart I will give you, and a new spirit I will put within you." (Ezekial 36:26)

• • •

"For I am sure that neither death, nor life, nor angels, nor principalities, nor things present, nor things to come, nor powers, nor height, nor depth, nor anything else in all creation, will be able to separate us from the love of God in Christ Jesus our Lord." (Romans 8:38-39)

• • •

The Memorial Service
A Sample Format for Clubs

Presiding Officer:
"It has been a tradition in the Federation that we pause at the beginning of our annual Convention for a few moments to remember and reflect on our members who have passed away during the last year."
•Prelude — appropriate music
•Prayer or responsive reading

Presiding Officer:
"Unfortunately, we have lost a number of wonderful members and friends."
•A short eulogy relating to the accomplishments of the deceased officers of the organization may precede the memorial roll call, depending on the size of the membership and the time allotted for the service.
•Music, a poem or a Bible verse may be presented at this time.
Presiding Officer: personal message
•Music/The Lord's Prayer
•A moment of silence
•The 23rd Psalm is recited in unison
•Benediction

Willamae M. Heitman, past president of the California State Federation of the National Association of Retired Federal Employees, conducted a beautiful memorial ceremony at the group's state convention.

Ms. Heitman shared her words of wisdom:

"In death there is certainly the very real pain and sorrow of physical separation. When our friends and loved ones die, they do not just go off to some dark and distant place. They simply begin their journey into eternity.

"I have often reflected upon this beautiful truth and found it the surest comfort in my personal time of mourning, that for us who believe, passing through death is really birth into a new and better world. Although we cannot deny the reality of death, as we know, death is part of life. Through our tears and sorrow, we can be comforted in the knowledge that death is a preparation for eternal union with those we love, in the peace and joy of heaven.

"Those who are left behind should not grieve as if there were no hope — may God help us all to realize that death is not the end, but the beginning of eternal life! For this promise, we can be grateful.

"We honor with a floral tribute the memory of all our members who have passed away during this past year."

(A solo, "The Lord's Prayer," concluded the service.)

• • •

THE TRAVELLER
He has put on invisibility
Dear Lord, I cannot see —
But this I know, although the road ascends
And passes from my sight,
That there will be no night;
That You will take him gently by the hand
And lead him on
Along the road of life that never ends,
And he will find it is not death but dawn.
I do not doubt that You are there as here,
And You will hold him dear.

Our life did not begin with birth,
It is not of the earth;
And this that we call death, it is no more
Than the opening and closing of a door —
And in Your house how many rooms must be
Beyond this one where we rest momently.

Dear Lord, I thank You for the faith that frees,
The love that knows it cannot lose its own;
The love that, looking through the shadows, sees
That You and he and I are ever one!
                                        —*James Dillet Freeman*

• • •

A CANDLE IN THE NIGHT
So very many people
Are like a candle in the night.
Their gentle, noiseless beauty
Is like a steady, burning light.

Though they be short and tine
Or shapely tapers tall and fair,
Around them beams a radiance
That brightens life and steals our care.

They do not sense the darkness
Because their self-effacing glow
Encircles them with beauty
That shines alike on friend or foe.

And so, I watch the candles
That banish darkness in the night,
Though they be short and tine
Or tapers tall with flames of light.

—*Mary Stoner Wine*

• • •

CHANGE

Aye, call it wishful thinking, if you will,
But in my heart the thought comes surging still
That life is more than mortal,
And death is but the portal
Through which we pass
Into a realm which, though it be unknown
To our poor sense, is part of Nature's own
Creation's not contained by our small sphere
But far transcends the little "now" and "here."

A seed must "die" ere it matures a tree;
And trees are not "destroyed" when felled they be
By axes, storms, decay or forest fires.
As planks, or logs, or humas each acquires
New life thereby...
The mountain fissures — crumbles — grinds to sand,
And seas engulf it, but again as land
It rises high
When eons pass and earth's convulsions thrust
The metamorphosed mud as stony crust
Into the sky.

So naught is lost, though all things change in form.
And death's no cruel "end," but Nature's norm:
Not darkness — light;
Not loss, but gain; not prison, but release
From pain, frustration, ignorance — to peace
Where all is bright.

Be not by mankinds ancient fears dismayed;
Walk to, and through, death's doorway unafraid.
                                        —*John J. Schuck*

THE LORD'S PRAYER
Our Father which art in heaven,
Hallowed be thy name.
Thy Kingdom come.
Thy will be done on earth
    as it is in heaven.
Give us this day our daily bread.
And forgive us our debts,
    as we forgive our debtors.
And lead us not into temptation,
    but deliver us from evil:
For thine is the kingdom,
    and the power,
    and the glory,
    forever. Amen.
(Matthew 6: 9-13)

•••

THE 23rd PSALM

The Lord is my shepherd; I shall not want.
He maketh me to lie down in green pastures:
He leadeth me beside the still waters.
He restoreth my soul: He leadeth me in the
　　paths of righteousness for His name's sake.
Yea, though I walk through the valley of
　　the shadow of death, I will fear no evil:
　　for thou art with me; Thy rod and
　　thy staff they comfort me.
Thou preparest a table before me in the presence
　　of mine enemies: thou anointest my head with oil;
　　my cup runneth over.
Surely goodness and mercy shall follow me
　　all the days of my life: and I will
　　dwell inthe house of the Lord forever.

● ● ●

Death is not the enemy of life, but its friend,
for it is the knowledge that our years are limited
which makes them so precious. It is the truth that
time is but lent to us which makes us, at our best,
look upon our years as a trust handed into our temporary
keeping.

—*Joshua Loth Liebman*

● ● ●

Additional Sources:

Salesian Missions publishes a beautiful booklet, "Coping,"
which contains many verses of prose and poetry suitable for
use at memorial services. These can be obtained for a donation
to Salesian Missions, 2 Lefevre Lane, New Rochelle, NY, 10801.

239

PART III
A Treasury of Reference Material

Chapter 12: Bible Texts
Chapter 13: Maxims — Life and Humor
Chapter 14: Gems of Wisdom

CHAPTER 12
Bible Texts

•Excerpts of Favorite Verses
Arranged in Topical Order

HEAR THE WORDS OF THE WISE
"Incline your ear, and hear the words of the wise,
and apply your mind to my knowledge;
for it will be pleasant if you keep them within you,
if all of them are ready on your lip.
That your trust may be in the Lord,
I have made them known to you today, even to you."
(Proverbs 22:17-19)

CHAPTER 12
Bible Texts

The following Bible verses were compiled to aid speakers and writers in their search for appropriate texts for specific topics.

Reading, studying and comprehending the Bible can be a life-long pilgrimage, and the dedicated student will undoubtedly have a large appendix to add to this abbreviated list.

Biblical quotations lend authority and credibility to the spoken and written word. Often just browsing through the Bible will bring to light the relevant verse to convey the message.

"For every one who asks receives, and he who seeks finds, and to him who knocks it will be opened." (Luke 11:10)

(All quotations in this chapter are taken from the Revised Standard Version of the Holy Bible (c) 1946, 1952, 1971, by Division of Christian Education of National Council of Churches of Christ in U.S.A., and used with permission.)

ABUNDANCE

And the Lord was with him; wherever he went forth, he prospered. (II Kings 18:7)

•••

Every one who asks receives. (Matthew 7:8)

•••

I will... reveal to them abundance of prosperity and security. (Jeremiah 33:6)

•••

Whatever you ask in my name, I will do it, that the Father may be glorified in the Son; if you ask anything in my name, I will do it. (John 14:13-14)

•••

Honor the Lord with your substance... then your barns will be filled with plenty. (Proverbs 3:9-10)

•••

Take delight in the Lord, and he will give you the desires of your heart. (Psalms 37:4)

ACHIEVEMENT

For whatever a man sows, that he will also reap.... Let us not grow weary in well-doing, for in due season we shall reap, if we do not lose heart. (Galatians 6:7,9)

•••

You will decide on a matter, and it will be established for you. (Job 22:28)

•••

With God all things are possible (Matthew 19:26)

•••

I can do all things in him who strengthens me. (Philippians 4:13)

•••

My help comes from the Lord, who made heaven and earth. (Psalms 121:2)

●●●

The Lord will fulfill his purpose for me. (Psalms 138:8) —

BELIEF

For as he thinketh in his heart, so is he. (Proverbs 23:7)

●●●

You are light in the Lord; walk as children of light. (Ephesians 5:8)

●●●

Do not fear; only believe. (Mark 5:36)

●●●

All authority in heaven and on earth has been given to me. (Matthew 28:18)

●●●

In God I trust without a fear. (Psalms 56:11)

BLESSINGS

I will send down the showers in their season; they shall be showers of blessings. (Ezekial 34:26)

●●●

May the God of hope fill you with all joy and peace in believing, so that by the power of the Holy Spirit you may abound in hope. (Romans 15:13)

●●●

The Lord bless you and keep you;
The Lord make his face to shine upon you
    and be gracious to you;
The Lord lift up his countenance upon you,
    and give you peace. (Numbers 6:24-26)

BROTHERHOOD
For whoever does the will of my Father in heaven is my brother, and sister, and mother. (Matthew 12:50)

• • •

So whatever you wish that men would do to you, do so to them. (Matthew 7:12)

• • •

By this all men will know that you are my disciples, if you have love for one another. (John 13:35)

• • •

This I command you, to love one another. (John 15:17)

• • •

You are no longer strangers and sojourners, but you are fellow citizens with the saints and members of the household of God. (Ephesians 2:19)

• • •

You shall love the Lord your God.... This is the great and first commandment. And a second is like it: you shall love your neighbor as yourself. (Matthew 22:37-39)

• • •

Practice hospitality. (Romans 12:13)

• • •

Be at peace among yourselves. (I Thessalonians 5:13)

COMFORT
I will fill this house with splendor, says the Lord. (Haggai 2:7)

• • •

Therefore comfort one another. (I Thessalonians 4:18)

• • •

I will not leave you comfortless: I will come to you. (John 14:18)

• • •

God abides in us and his love is perfected in us. By this we know that we abide in him and he in us, because he has given us of his own Spirit. (I John 4:12-13)

• • •

This God — his way is perfect; the promise of the Lord proves true. (II Samuel 22:31)

• • •

Thou dost keep him in perfect peace, whose mind is stayed on thee. (Isaiah 26:3)

• • •

He who sent me is with me; he has not left me alone. (John 8:29)

• • •

It is the Lord who goes before you; he will be with you, he will not fail you or forsake you; do not fear or be dismayed. (Deuteronomy 31:8)

• • •

My presence will go with you, and I will give you rest. (Exodus 33:14)

• • •

The eternal God is your dwelling place, and underneath are the everlasting arms. (Deuteronomy 33:27)

• • •

Blessed be the God and Father of our Lord Jesus Christ, the Father of mercies and God of all comfort. (II Corinthians 1:3)

COURAGE
Be of good courage. (Numbers 13:20)

• • •

Be strong, and let your heart take courage; yea, wait for the Lord! (Psalms 27:14)

• • •

In returning and rest you shall be saved; in quietness and in trust shall be your strength. (Isaiah 30:15)

• • •

By this we know that we abide in him and he in us, because he has given us of his own Spirit. (I John 4:13)

• • •

Be strong and of good courage; do not fear or be in dread of them: for it is the Lord your God who goes with you; he will not fail you or forsake you. (Deuteronomy 31:6)

DIVINE ORDER

For everything there is a season and a time for every matter under heaven. (Ecclesiastes 3:1)

• • •

All things should be done decently and in order. (I Corinthians 14:40)

• • •

His delight is in the law of the Lord, and on his law he meditates day and night. (Psalms 1:2)

• • •

Thou hast established the earth, and it stands fast... for all things are thy servants. (Psalms 119:90-91)

• • •

The heavens are telling the glory of God; and the firmament proclaims his handiwork. (Psalms 19:1)

• • •

DOMINION

All power is given unto me in heaven and in earth. (Matthew 28:18)

● ● ●

You shall receive power when the Holy Spirit has come upon you. (Acts 1:8)

● ● ●

A new heart I will give you, and a new spirit I will put within you. (Ezekial 36:26)

● ● ●

But as for me, I am filled with power, with the Spirit of the Lord. (Micah 3:8)

● ● ●

For freedom Christ has set us free; stand fast therefore, and do not submit again to a yoke of slavery. (Galatians 5:1)

FAITH

If you have faith as a grain of mustard seed, you will say to this mountain, "Move from here to there," and it will move; and nothing will be impossible to you. (Matthew 17:20)

● ● ●

Great is your faith! Be it done for you as you desire. (Matthew 15:28)

● ● ●

Your faith has made you well. (Matthew 9:22)

● ● ●

And whatever you ask in prayer, you will receive, if you have faith. (Matthew 21:22)

● ● ●

If you can! All things are possible to him who believes. (Mark 9:23)

● ● ●

The Lord is my light and my salvation; whom shall I fear? (Psalms 27:1)

• • •

If you have faith and never doubt... even if you say to this mountain, "Be taken up and cast into the sea," it will be done. (Matthew 21:21)

• • •

Now faith is the assurance of things hoped for, the conviction of things not seen... By faith we understand that the world was created by the word of God, so that what is seen was made out of things which do not appear. (Hebrews 11:1-3)

• • •

Since we have the same spirit of faith as he had who wrote, "I believed, and so I spoke," we too believe, and so we speak. (II Corinthians 4:13)

• • •

Through whom we have received grace and apostleship to bring about the obedience of faith for the sake of his name among all the nations. (Romans 1:5)

• • •

According to the riches of his glory, he may grant you to be strengthened with might through his Spirit in the inner man, and that Christ may dwell in your hearts through faith. (Ephesians 3:16-17)

FEAR
In God I trust without a fear. (Psalms 56:11)

• • •

I sought the Lord, and he answered me, and delivered me from all my fears. (Psalms 34:4)

• • •

Fear not, for I am with you. (Genesis 26:24)

•••

The Lord is my light and my salvation; whom shall I fear? (Psalms 27:1)

•••

There is no fear in love, but perfect love casts out fear. (I John 4:18)

FORGIVENESS

Judge not, and you will not be judged; condemn not, and you will not be condemned; forgive, and you will be forgiven. (Luke 6:37)

•••

Lord, how often shall my brother sin against me and I forgive him? "I do not say to you seven times, but seventy times seven." (Matthew 18:21-22)

•••

The Son of man has authority on earth to forgive sins. (Matthew 9:6)

•••

Whenever you stand praying, forgive, if you have anything against any one. (Mark 11:25)

FREEDOM

If you continue in my word, you are truly my disciples, and you will know the truth, and the truth will make you free. (John 8:31-32)

•••

Live as free men, yet without using your freedom as a pretext for evil, but live as servants of God. (I Peter 2:16)

•••

For freedom Christ has set us free; stand fast therefore, and do not submit again to a yoke of slavery. (Galatians 5:1)

•••

I shall walk at liberty, for I have sought thy precepts. (Psalms 119:45)

•••

Be strong in the Lord. (Ephesians 6:10)

GIFTS

Every good endowment and every perfect gift is from above. (James 1:17)

•••

Yea, the Lord will give what is good, and our land will yield its increase. (Psalms 85:12)

•••

Give, and it will be given to you; good measure, pressed down, shaken together, running over, will be put into your lap. For the measure you give will be the measure you get back. (Luke 6:38)

GLORY

And my God will supply every need of yours according to his riches in glory in Christ Jesus. (Philippians 4:19)

•••

Let your light so shine before men, that they may see your good works and give glory to your Father who is in heaven. (Matthew 5:16)

GOD'S PRESENCE

The wind blows where it wills, and you hear the sound of it, but you do not know whence it comes or whither it goes; so it is with everyone who is born of the Spirit. (John 3:8)

•••

My grace is sufficient for you, for my power is made perfect in weakness. (II Corinthians 12:9)

• • •

The blessing of the Lord be upon you! We bless you in the name of the Lord! (Psalms 129:8)

• • •

The Lord is just in all his ways, and kind in all his doings. (Psalms 145:17)

• • •

My presence will go with you, and I will give you rest. (Exodus 33:14)

• • •

Be still, and know that I am God. (Psalms 46:10)

GOODNESS

Do not be conformed to this world, but be transformed by the renewal of your mind, that you may prove what is the will of God, what is good and acceptable and perfect. (Romans 12:2)

• • •

In everything God works for good with those who love him. (Romans 8:28)

• • •

Surely goodness and mercy shall follow me all the days of my life; and I shall dwell in the house of the Lord forever. (Psalms 23:6)

• • •

The Lord is good to those who wait for him. (Lamentations 3:25)

• • •

GUIDANCE

I will instruct you and teach you the way you should go; I will counsel you with my eye upon you. (Psalms 32:8)

•••

Make me to know Thy ways, O Lord; teach me Thy paths. Lead me in Thy truth, and teach me, for thou art the God of my salvation. (Psalms 25:4-5)

•••

In paths that they have not known I will guide them. (Isaiah 42:16)

•••

In all your ways acknowledge him, and he will make straight your paths. (Proverbs 3:6)

HARMONY

And above all these put on love, which binds everything together in perfect harmony. And let the peace of Christ rule in your hearts. (Colossians 3:14-15)

•••

If two of you agree on earth about anything they ask, it will be done for them by my Father in heaven. (Matthew 18:19)

•••

Be kind to one another, tenderhearted, forgiving to one another, as God in Christ forgave you. (Ephesians 4:32)

•••

Live in harmony with one another. (Romans 12:16)

•••

And he awoke and rebuked the wind and the raging waves; and they ceased, and there was a calm. (Luke 8:24)

•••

HEALING

The spirit of God has made me, and the breath of the Almighty gives me life. (Job 33:4)

• • •

Your faith has made you well; go in peace, and be healed. (Mark 5:34)

• • •

The power of the Lord was with him to heal. (Luke 5:17)

• • •

Bless the Lord, O my soul... who heals all your diseases. (Psalms 103:2-3)

• • •

The God of all grace, who has called you to his eternal glory in Christ, will himself restore, establish and strengthen you. (I Peter 5:10)

• • •

He will renew you in his love. (Zeph. 3:17)

• • •

The tongue of the wise brings healing. (Proverbs 12:18)

• • •

Your faith has made you well. (Matthew 9:22)

• • •

For I will restore to you, and your wounds I will heal, says the Lord. (Jeremiah 30:17)

HEALTH

A cheerful heart is a good medicine, but a downcast spirit dries up the bones. (Proverbs 17:22)

• • •

And let steadfastness have its full effect, that you may be perfect and complete, lacking in nothing. (James 1:4)

• • •

With thee is the fountain of life. (Psalms 36:9)

•••

They shall mount up with wings like eagles, they shall run and not be weary, they shall walk and not faint. (Isaiah 40:31)

•••

A tranquil mind gives life to the flesh. (Proverbs 14:30)

•••

If then your whole body is full of light, having no part dark, it will be wholly bright. (Luke 11:36)

•••

Cast all your anxieties on him, for he cares about you. (I Peter 5:7)

•••

Come away by yourselves... and rest awhile. (Mark 6:31)

•••

The whole body, nourished and knit together through its joints and ligaments, grows with a growth that is from God. (Colossians 2:19)

•••

If there is a physical body, there is also a spiritual body. (I Corinthians 15:44)

ILLUMINATION

For now we see in a mirror dimly, but then face to face. Now I know in part; then I shall understand fully. (I Corinthians 13:12)

•••

But it is the spirit in a man, the breath of the Almighty, that makes him understand. (Job 32:8)

•••

God is light and in him is no darkness at all. (I John 1:5)

•••

We look not to things that are seen but to the things that are unseen; for the things that are seen are transient, but the things that are unseen are eternal. (II Corinthians 4:18)

INSTRUCTION
I will instruct you and teach you the way you should go. (Psalms 32:8)

●●●

But the wisdom from above is first pure, then peaceable, gentle, open to reason, full of mercy and good fruits, without uncertainty or insincerity. (James 3:17)

●●●

If I take the wings of the morning and dwell in the uttermost parts of the sea, even there thy hand shall lead me. (Psalms 139:9-10)

●●●

Let thy good spirit lead me on a level path! (Psalms 143:10)

●●●

And your ears shall hear a word behind you, saying, "This is the way, walk in it." (Isaiah 30:21)

JOY
Everlasting joy shall be upon their heads; they shall obtain joy and gladness. (Isaiah 51:11)

●●●

Make a joyful noise to the Lord, all the lands! Come into his presence with singing! (Psalms 100:1-2)

●●●

O sing to the Lord a new song, for he has done marvelous things! (Psalms 98:1)

●●●

Rejoice in that day, and leap for joy, for behold, your reward is great in heaven. (Luke 6:23)

•••

Ask, and you will receive, that your joy may be full. (John 16:24)

•••

They shall obtain joy and gladness, and sorrow and sighing shall flee away. (Isaiah 35:10)

JUSTICE

And what does the Lord require of you but to do justice and to love kindness? (Micah 6:8)

•••

Render true judgements, show kindness and mercy. (Zachariah 7:9)

•••

Hold fast to love and justice, and wait continually for your God. (Hosea 12:6)

•••

Justice, and only justice, you shall follow. (Deuteronomy 16:20)

LIGHT

Come, let us walk in the light of the Lord. (Isaiah 2:5)

•••

Your eye is the lamp of your body; when your eye is sound, your whole body is full of light. (Luke 11:34)

•••

Put on the armor of light. (Romans 13:12)

•••

You are light in the Lord; walk as children of light. (Ephesians 5:8)

LOVE

And above all these things put on love, which binds everything together in perfect harmony. (Colossians 3:14)

• • •

And it is my prayer that your love may abound more and more. (Philippians 1:9)

• • •

Love bears all things, believes all things, hopes all things, endures all things. (I Corinthians 13:7)

• • •

So faith, hope, love abide, these three; but the greatest of these is love. (I Corinthians 13:13)

• • •

A new commandment I give to you, that you love one another; even as I have loved you, that you also love one another. (John 13:34)

• • •

This is my commandment, that you love one another as I have loved you. (John 15:12)

• • •

Love is patient and kind. (I Corinthians 13:4)

• • •

There is no fear in love, but perfect love casts out fear. (I John 4:18)

NEW DAY

Weeping may tarry for the night, but joy comes with the morning. (Psalms 30:5)

• • •

Awake, O sleeper, and arise. (Ephesians 5:14)

• • •

Behold, now is the acceptable time; behold, now is the day of salvation. (II Corinthians 6:2)

• • •

Therefore, if anyone is in Christ, he is a new creation; the old has passed away, behold, the new has come. (II Corinthians 5:17)

• • •

Choose this day whom you will serve. (Joshua 24:15)

• • •

Behold, I send you out as sheep in the midst of wolves; so be wise as serpents and innocent as doves. (Matthew 10:16)

ONENESS

My presence will go with you. (Exodus 33:14)

• • •

In him we live and move and have our being. (Acts 17:28)

• • •

Little children, you are of God, and have overcome them; for he who is in you is greater than he who is in the world. (I John 4:4)

• • •

The eternal God is your dwelling place, and underneath are the everlasting arms. (Deuteronomy 33:27)

• • •

In him you also... were sealed with the promised Holy Spirit, which is the guarantee of our inheritance. (Ephesians 1:13-14)

• • •

Am I a God at hand, says the Lord, and not a God afar off? (Jeremiah 23:23)

• • •

Be still and know that I am God. (Psalms 46:10)

• • •

PATIENCE

The Lord is good to those who wait for him. (Lamentations 3:25)

• • •

Be patient. (James 5:7)

• • •

The trying of your faith worketh patience. But let patience have her perfect work. (James 1:3-4)

• • •

They are those who, hearing the word, hold it fast in an honest and good heart, and bring forth fruit with patience. (Luke 8:15)

• • •

I tell you, do not be anxious. (Matthew 6:25)

PEACE

Lead a life worthy of the calling... eager to maintain the unity of the Spirit in the bond of peace. (Ephesians 4:1-3)

• • •

Peace I leave with you; my peace I give to you; not as the world gives do I give to you. Let not your hearts be troubled. (John 14:27)

• • •

Be at peace among yourselves. (I Thessalonians 5:13)

• • •

Blessed are the peacemakers, for they shall be called sons of God. (Matthew 5:9)

• • •

The God of peace will be with you. (Philippians 4:9)

• • •

Thou dost keep him in perfect peace, whose mind is stayed on thee, because he trusts in thee. (Isaiah 26:3)

• • •

263

For God is not a God of confusion but of peace. (I Corinthians 14:33)

•••

Let us then pursue what makes for peace and for mutual upbuilding. (Romans 14:19)

•••

Great peace have those who love thy law; nothing can make them stumble. (Psalms 119:165)

POSITIVE ATTITUDE

Do not judge by appearances. (John 7:24)

•••

You will decide on a matter, and it will be established for you, and light will shine on your ways. (Job 22:28)

•••

Judge not... condemn not. (Luke 6:37)

•••

For as he thinketh in his heart, so is he. (Proverbs 23:7)

•••

In God I trust without a fear. (Psalms 56:4)

•••

Look at the ships, also; though they are so great and are driven by strong winds, they are guided by a very small rudder wherever the will of the pilot directs. (James 3:4)

•••

Do not be conformed to this world but be transformed by the renewal of your mind, that you may prove what is the will of God, what is good and acceptable and perfect. (Romans 12:2)

PRAISE

Finally, brethren, whatever is true, whatever is honorable, whatever is just, whatever is pure, whatever is lovely, whatever is gracious... think about these things. (Philippians 4:8)

• • •

Praise the Lord! O give thanks to the Lord, for he is good; for his steadfast love endures forever! (Psalms 106:1)

• • •

Make a joyful noise to God, all the earth; sing the glory of his name; give to him glorious praise! (Psalms 66:1-2)

• • •

Let everything that breathes praise the Lord! Praise the Lord! (Psalms 150:6)

• • •

I will praise the name of God with a song; I will magnify him with thanksgiving. (Psalms 69:30)

PRAYER

Therefore I tell you, whatever you ask in prayer, believe that you have received it, and it will be yours. (Mark 11:24)

• • •

Pray for one another, that you may be healed. The prayer of a righteous man has great power in its effects. (James 5:16)

• • •

But when you pray, go into your room and shut the door and pray to your Father who is in secret; and your Father who sees in secret will reward you. (Matthew 6:6)

• • •

Let the words of my mouth and the meditation of my heart be acceptable in thy sight, O Lord, my rock and my redeemer. (Psalms 19:14)

•••

Without ceasing I mention you always in my prayers. (Romans 1:9)

PROTECTION
Be strong and of good courage, do not fear or be in dread of them: for it is the Lord your God who goes with you; he will not fail you or forsake you. (Deuteronomy 31:6)

•••

He who dwells in the shelter of the Most High... will say to the Lord, "My refuge and my fortress; my God, in whom I trust." (Psalms 91:1-2)

•••

The Lord is good, a stronghold in the day of trouble; he knows those who take refuge in him. (Nahum 1:7)

•••

In peace I will both lie down and sleep; for thou alone, O Lord, makest me dwell in safety. (Psalms 4:8)

REJOICE
Happy is he who trusts in the Lord. (Proverbs 16:20)

•••

You shall be happy, and it shall be well with you. (Psalms 128:2)

•••

I will greatly rejoice in the Lord, my soul shall exult in my God. (Isaiah 61:10)

•••

This is the day which the Lord has made; let us rejoice and be glad in it. (Psalms 118:24)

•••

Rejoice always, pray constantly, give thanks in all circumstances; for this is the will of God in Christ Jesus for you. (I Thessalonians 5:16-18)

You shall rejoice... in all that you undertake, in which the Lord your God has blessed you. (Deuteronomy 12:7)

STRENGTH

God is our refuge and strength, a very present help in trouble. (Psalms 46:1)

•••

The Lord God is my strength and my song, and he has become my salvation. (Isaiah 12:2)

•••

For God alone my soul waits in silence, for my hope is from him. He only is my rock and my salvation, my fortress; I shall not be shaken. (Psalms 62:5-6)

•••

But as for me, I am filled with power, with the Spirit of the Lord. (Micah 3:8)

•••

They who wait for the Lord shall renew their strength, they shall mount up with wings like eagles, they shall run and not be weary. (Isaiah 40:31)

•••

SUCCESS

If two of you agree on earth about anything they ask, it will be done for them by my Father in heaven. (Matthew 18:19)

• • •

I am sure that he who began a good work in you will bring it to completion. (Philippians 1:6)

• • •

I know that thou canst do all things, and that no purpose of thine can be thwarted. (Job 42:2)

• • •

I know how to abound; in any and all circumstances I have learned the secret.... I can do all things in him who strengthens me. (Philippians 4:12-13)

• • •

All that the Father has is mine; therefore I said that he will take what is mine and declare it to you. (John 16:15)

TRUST

Trust in him at all times, O people; pour out your heart before him; God is a refuge for us. (Psalms 62:8)

• • •

We have confidence before God; and we receive from him whatever we ask. (I John 3:21-22)

• • •

Behold, God is my salvation; I will trust, and will not be afraid. (Isaiah 12:2)

• • •

Trust in the Lord with all your heart... In all your ways acknowledge him and he will make straight your paths. (Proverbs 3:5-6)

• • •

He who trusts in the Lord is safe. (Proverbs 29:25)

WISDOM
The beginning of wisdom is this: Get wisdom, and whatever you get, get insight. (Proverbs 4:7)

• • •

If any of you lacks wisdom, let him ask God. (James 1:5)

• • •

An intelligent mind acquires knowledge, and the ear of the wise seeks knowledge. (Proverbs 18:15)

• • •

Behold, thou desirest truth in the inward being; therefore teach me wisdom in my secret heart. (Psalms 51:6)

• • •

Happy is the man who finds wisdom, and the man who gets understanding. (Proverbs 3:13)

• • •

The Lord will guide you continually. (Isaiah 58:11)

WORDS
And the Lord said to me, "Behold, I have put my words in your mouth. (Jeremiah 1:9)

• • •

...for by your words you will be justified, and by your words you will be condemned. (Matthew 12:37)

• • •

Pleasant words are like a honeycomb, sweetness to the soul and health to the body. (Proverbs 16:24)

• • •

The words that I have spoken to you are spirit and life. (John 6:63)

• • •

Let your speech always be gracious. (Colossians 4:6)

•••

WORKS
Show me your faith apart from your works, and I by my works will show you my faith. (James 2:18)

•••

Do whatever your hand finds to do, for God is with you. (I Samuel 10:7)

•••

Commit your work to the Lord, and your plans will be established. (Proverbs 16:3)

•••

As we have opportunity, let us do good to all men. (Galatians 6:10)

•••

We know that in everything God works for good with those who love him. (Romans 8:28)

WORLD PEACE
Blessed are the peacemakers, for they shall be called sons of God. (Matthew 5:9)

•••

Live peaceably with all. (Romans 12:18)

•••

Finally, all of you, have a unity of spirit, sympathy, love of the brethren, a tender heart and a humble mind. (I Peter 3:8)

•••

Lead a life worthy of the calling to which you have been called, with all lowliness and meekness, with patience forbearing one another in love, eager to maintain the unity of the

Spirit in the bond of peace. (Ephesians 4:1-3)

• • •

Love one another earnestly from the heart. You have been born anew... through the living and abiding word of God. (I Peter 1:22-23)

• • •

Behold, how good and pleasant it is when brothers dwell in unity! (Psalms 133:1)

• • •

Glory to God in the highest, and on earth peace among men with whom he is pleased. (Luke 2:14)

• • •

He shall command peace to the nations; his dominion shall be from sea to sea. (Zechariah 9:10)

• • •

For he is our peace, who has made us both one, and has broken down the dividing wall... Through him we both have access in one Spirit to the Father. (Ephesians 2:14,18)

• • •

There is no distinction... the same Lord is Lord of all and bestows his riches upon all who call upon him. (Romans 10:12)

• • •

CHAPTER 13
Maxims: Life and Humor

•Closing thoughts for newsletters, church bulletins, speakers and writers.

*Sprinkle in a few maxims to stir your audience's
perspective and add a touch of humor.*

CHAPTER 13
Maxims: Life and Humor

For closing thoughts, monthly magazines, newsletters, church bulletins and also for speakers and writers.

The following are sparks of truth and humor that were included to help make "Good Graces" a one-stop shopping oasis for either verbal or written philosophical or religious material.

Many organizations have monthly magazines with harried editors looking for fillers. These maxims may help supply the filler space needed and give the readership a chuckle. A "Chaplain's Corner" could add interest to the publication. Readers Digest would certainly vouch for the popularity of one-liners.

Church billboards have found thought-provoking or snappy sentences an effective means for luring outsiders into the inner sanctum, to increase attendance.

These axioms are gleaned from a variety of sources, and credit to the author is given when known. We offer a sincere "thanks" to them, and also the authors of the anonymous works.

"All the good maxims have been written. It only remains to put them into practice." —*B. Pascal*

AXIOMS AND POINTS TO PONDER
These familiar and some unfamiliar quotations are included for reference material.

Also, these salient ideas will be beneficial when preparing speeches for any type of assembly.

Trying to put these axioms in a logical order seemed like a logical thing to do. But viewing the task realistically, a logical order would differ according to each person's insight.

Therefore, your indulgence is requested on the index-sequence of this material. Locating the just-right sentence may present a challenge, but look at it this way: *"Have patience. All things are difficult before they become easy."* —*Saadi*.

"A word fitly spoken is like apples of gold in a setting of silver." (Proverbs 25:11)

• • •

"A good scare is worth more to a man than good advice."
—*E.W. Howe*

• • •

"There is nothing so ridiculous that has not at some time been said by some philosopher." —*Oliver Goldsmith*

• • •

"If you wouldn't write it, don't say it."

• • •

"Consider how hard it is to change yourself and you'll understand   what little chance you have trying to change others."

—*Arnold Glascow*

• • •

"No vice is so bad as advice."

• • •

"You can preach a better sermon with your life than with you lips."

—*Oliver Goldsmith*

• • •

"Food for thought is usually hard to digest."

• • •

"Only hens bear dividends by sitting around."

• • •

"A man would do nothing if he waited until he could do it so well that no one would find fault with what he has done."

—*Cardinal Newman*

• • •

"Whether you believe you can do a thing or not, you are right."

—*Henry Ford*

• • •

"The man who really wants to accomplish something finds a way. The man who doesn't finds an excuse."

—*Wes Izzard*

• • •

"Nothing great was ever achieved without enthusiasm."

—*Ralph Waldo Emerson*

• • •

"The man who does things makes many mistakes, but he never makes the biggest mistake of all — doing nothing."

—*Benjamin Franklin*

• • •

"Swallowing angry words is much easier than having to eat them."

• • •

"If you borrow trouble, no one wants it back."

• • •

"A youthful spirit keeps a man young at heart."

• • •

"Of all the things you wear, your expression is the most important."

• • •

"An optimist is wrong as often as a pessimist, but far happier."

• • •

"When an optimist gets the worst of it, he makes the best of it."

• • •

"One way to break a bad habit is to drop it."

• • •

"Cheerfulness is what greases the axles of the world."

• • •

"Those who look ahead show they have one."

• • •

"Character is what we are in the dark."

• • •

"Character makes the poor man rich."

• • •

"Reputation is what men think we are. Character is what God sees we are."

• • •

"Toot the other guy's horn for awhile to give yours a rest."

• • •

"To escape criticism: Say nothing, do nothing, be nothing."

"The trouble with most of us is that we would rather be ruined by praise than saved by criticism."

• • •

"A gentleman is a man who can disagree without being disagreeable."

• • •

"Be patient with the faults of others; they have to be patient with yours."

• • •

"Always start with the assumption that your critics may be right."

• • •

"I'm grateful to my enemies. In the long range movement toward progress, a kick in the pants sends you further along than a friendly handshake."

—David Sarnoff

• • •

"Whatever you dislike in another person, be sure to correct in yourself."

• • •

"Bad habits are like a comfortable bed; easy to get into, but hard to get out of."

• • •

"If fate hands you a lemon, don't squeeze it — make lemonade."

• • •

"Swallowing false pride will never give one indigestion."

• • •

"Visits always give pleasure — if not the arrival, the departure."

• • •

"The surest way to get rid of an enemy is to make a friend of him."

279

• • •

"The only way to have a friend is to be one."

—Emerson

• • •

"Strangers are friends you haven't met."

• • •

"Careless words make friends care less."

• • •

"Friends are priceless; don't sell them short."

• • •

"A friend in need is usually avoided."

• • •

"One who uses a friend can lose a friend."

• • •

"When you throw mud, your hands get dirty."

• • •

"If you want a good neighbor, be one."

• • •

"Nothing is gained by winning an argument and losing a friend."

• • •

"Enemies are really friends in disguise — they keep us on our toes."

• • •

"All men who disagree with you are not wrong."

• • •

"He who forgives ends the quarrel."

• • •

"Be kind — for everyone you meet is fighting a hard battle."

• • •

"You can hardly make a friend in a year, but you can easily lose one in an hour."

● ● ●

"Woe unto you, when all men shall speak well of you."

● ● ●

"You probably wouldn't worry about what people think of you if you knew how seldom they did."

● ● ●

"A friend is one who knows all about you, and likes you just the same."

● ● ●

"You must have long-range goals to keep you from being frustrated by short-range failures."

—*C. Noble*

● ● ●

"You won't ever get started if you wait for all the conditions to be just right."

● ● ●

"Big shots are only little shots who kept shooting."

—*Christopher Morley*

● ● ●

"A mediocre plan, well executed, is better than an excellent plan, poorly executed."

—*Napoleon*

● ● ●

"The man who makes no mistakes does not usually make anything."

● ● ●

"You can't hold a man down without staying down with him."

—*Booker T. Washington*

● ● ●

"Happiness is not something you find, but something you create."

281

"To miss the joy is to miss all."

—*Robert Louis Stevenson*

• • •

"We judge ourselves by what we think we can do. Others judge us by what we have already done."

—*Seneca*

• • •

"The measure of a man's real character is what he would do if he knew he would never be found out."

—*Macauley*

• • •

"When two men always agree on everything, one of them is doing all the thinking."

—*S. Rayburn*

• • •

"There is so much good in the worst of us,
And so much bad in the best of us,
That it ill behooves any of us
To speak ill of the rest of us."

• • •

"The man who says nothing at the right time is a good talker."

• • •

"Great minds discuss ideas; average minds discuss events; small minds discuss people."

• • •

"When you talk, you repeat what you already know; when you listen, you often learn something."

—*Sparks*

• • •

"Man's mind, stretched to a new idea, never goes back to its original dimension."

—*Oliver Wendell Holmes*

•••

"The best way to get even is to forget."

•••

"It isn't what we have, but what we are, that makes life worth living."

•••

A good leader takes a little more than his share of blame; a little less than his share of credit."

—*Arnold Glascow*

•••

"The secret of patience is doing something else in the meantime."

•••

"The frightening fact about heredity and environment is that we parents provide both."

•••

"He who is afraid of asking is afraid of knowing."

•••

"So live that you need not be afraid of tomorrow nor ashamed of yesterday."

•••

"Man is the only animal that blushes — or needs to."

•••

"He who laughs last didn't catch on very fast."

•••

"Some give pleasure when they enter a room; others when they leave it."

•••

"We see things not as they are, but as we are." —*Tomlinson*

•••

"Leaders are ordinary persons with extraordinary determinations."

•••

"The reason a lot of people cannot find Opportunity is it goes about disguised as Hard Work."

• • •

"Put work into life, and life into your work."

• • •

"There are no elevators in the house of success; you must toil up one step at a time."

• • •

"The man who wakes up and finds himself famous hasn't been asleep."

• • •

"Nobody knows the age of the human race, but all agree it is old enough to know better."

• • •

"You can't change the past, but you can ruin a perfectly good present by worrying over the future."

• • •

"If a thing will go without saying, let it go."

• • •

"Everyone can do something to make the world better. He can at least improve himself."

• • •

"When a door is shut, another is open."

—*Cervantes*

• • •

"A heel never toes the mark."

• • •

"Give some people an inch, and they act like a ruler."

• • •

"Public opinion is what people think people think."

• • •

"The trouble with the world today is a lack of vision for

tomorrow."

• • •

"Silence is one of the hardest arguments to refute."

—Sochatt

• • •

"Let your speech be better than silence, or be silent."

• • •

"A man often repents that he has spoken, but seldom that he has held his tongue."

—Fuller

• • •

"I found out early in life that I never had to explain anything I hadn't said."

—Calvin Coolidge

• • •

"Empty wagons make the most noise."

• • •

"The three Bs of public speaking are: be brief, be bright and begone."

• • •

"If you never stick your neck out, you'll never get your head above the crowd."

• • •

"A person who aims at nothing usually hits it."

• • •

"He who has failed to prepare had better be prepared to fail."

• • •

"Success is never final — failure never fatal."

• • •

"Success is getting what you want; happiness is wanting what you get."

• • •

"It is unfortunate to have more dollars than sense."

• • •

"Wisdom is knowing what to do;
        Skill is knowing how to do it;
                Virtue is doing it."

• • •

"Frankness is often rudeness in disguise."

• • •

"A good conversationalist is one who is tolerant of your opinions."

• • •

"A truth that's told with bad intent
        Beats all the lies you can invent."

• • •

"It's easier to do a job right than to explain why you can't."
—*Martin Van Buren*

• • •

"Grumblers don't work; workers don't grumble. The mule can't kick and pull at the same time."

• • •

"The only substitute for work is a miracle."

• • •

"The best place to find a helping hand is at the end of your arm."

• • •

"Eggs and oaths are most often broken."

• • •

"What we are is God's gift to us; what we make of ourselves is our gift to God."

CHAPTER 14
Gems of Wisdom

- Ancient and present ideas to capture immortality.

CHAPTER 14
Gems of Wisdom

Down through the ages, timeless spiritual truths have been spoken by illumined souls who have walked the face of this earth.

These recorded pearls belie any boundaries of space, time, age or creed and are contemporary and universal in scope, bringing immortality into the present.

When enlightened words are so supercharged with truth, we have to take their revelations in small doses to assimilate the full content.

The depth of genius is not distilled until it has the stamp of history for authority.

Borrowing ideas and words from the works of great thinkers, literary giants and masters of the past add enrichment to our lives and provides the spark for today, the fire for tomorrow and the light for eternity.

THE EPISTLE OF PAUL THE
APOSTLE TO THE CORINTHIANS

1. Though I speak with the tongues of men and of angels, and have not charity, I am become as sounding brass, or a tinkling cymbal.

2. And though I have the gift of prophecy, and understand all mysteries, and all knowledge, and though I could remove mountains, and have not charity, I am nothing.

3. And though I bestow all my goods to feed the poor, and though I give my body to be burned, and have not charity, it profiteth me nothing.

13. And now abideth faith, hope, charity, these three; but the greatest of these is charity. (I Corinthians 1-3, 13) (KJV)

WHAT GOD IS LIKE
I did not know what God is like
Until a friendly word
Came to me in an hour of need.

I did not know what God is like
Until I heard love's feet
On errands of God's mercy
Go up and down life's street.

I did not know what God is like
Until I felt a hand
Clasp mine and lift me when alone
I had no strength to stand.

I think I know what God is like
For I have seen the face
Of God's son looking at me
From all the human race.

—James Dillet Freeman
(Printed with permission from the book, "What God is Like" by Mr. Freeman, (c) 1973 Unity School of Christianity)

• • •

"Place yourself in the middle of the stream of power and wisdom which flows into you as life, place yourself in the full center of that flood, and you are without effort impelled to truth, to right, and a perfect contentment."

—*Ralph Waldo Emerson*

• • •

If there is right in the soul,
There will be beauty in the person,
If there is beauty in the person,
There will be harmony in the home;
If there is harmony in the home,
There will be order in the nation;
If there is order in the nation,
There will be peace in the world.

—*Confucius*

• • •

I believe in God, who is for me spirit, love, the principle of all things.

I believe that God is in me, as I am in Him.

I believe that the true welfare of man consists in fulfilling the will of God.

I believe that from the fulfillment of the will of God, there can follow nothing but that which is good for me and for all men.

I believe that the will of God is that every man should love his fellow men, and should act toward others as he desired that they act toward him.

I believe that the reason of life is for each of us simply to grow in love.

I believe that this growth in love will contribute more than any other force to establish the Kingdom of God on earth.

—*Leo Tolstoy*

291

"I am now in the presence of pure Being, and immersed in the Holy Spirit of life, love and wisdom.

I acknowledge Thy presence and Thy power, O blessed Spirit; in Thy divine wisdom now erase my mortal limitations and from Thy pure substance of love bring into manifestation my world, according to Thy perfect law."

—Charles Fillmore

• • •

"Far better it is to dare mighty things, to win glorious triumphs, even though checkered by failure, than to take rank with those poor spirits who neither enjoy much or suffer much, because they live in the gray twilight that knows neither victory nor defeat."

—Theodore Roosevelt

• • •

And Moses said: "Hear, O Israel: the Lord our God is one Lord: And thou shalt love the Lord thy God with all thine heart, and with all thy soul, and with all thy might."(Deut. 6:4,5)

• • •

And Jesus answered him, "The first of all the commandments is, 'Hear, O Israel; the Lord our God is one Lord:

And thou shalt love the Lord thy God with all thy heart, and with all thy soul, and with all thy mind, and with all thy strength: this is the first commandment.

And the second is like, namely this, Thou shalt love thy neighbor as thyself. There is none other commandment greater than these. (Mark 12:29-31)(KJV)

• • •

LOVE

Love is an essence, an atmosphere, which defies analysis, as does Life Itself.

Love is the central Flame of the universe, nay, the very Fire Itself.

Love fires the heart, stimulates the emotions, renews the soul and proclaims the Spirit. —*Ernest Holmes*

• • •

Owe no man anything, but to love one another; for he that loveth another hath fulfilled the law. For this, Thou shalt not commit adultery, Thou shalt not kill, Thou shalt not steal, Thou shalt not bear false witness, Thou shalt not covet; and if there be any other commandment, it is briefly comprehended in this by saying, namely, Thou shalt love thy neighbor as thyself.

Love worketh no ill to his neighbor: therefore love is the fulfilling of the law. (Romans 13:8-10) (KJV)

• • •

Listen to the exhortation of the dawn!
    Look to this day!
For it is life, the very life of life.
In its brief course lie all the
Verities and realities of your existence;
    The bliss of growth,
    The glory of action,
    The splendor of beauty;
For yesterday is but a dream,
And tomorrow is only a vision;
    But today, well lived, makes
Every yesterday a dream of happiness,
And every tomorrow a vision of hope.
Look well therefore to this day!

—*A passage from the Sanskrit*

I find the great thing in this world is not so much where we stand, as in what direction we are moving. To reach the port of heaven, we must sail sometimes with the wind, and sometimes against it; but we must sail, and not drift, nor lie at anchor.

—*Oliver Wendell Holmes*

• • •

To give life a meaning, one must have a purpose larger than one's self.

—*Will Durant*

• • •

This above all: to thine own self be true,
And it must follow, as night the day,
Thou canst not then be false to any man.

—*William Shakespeare*

• • •

If it is a virtue to love my neighbor as a human being, it must be a virtue — and not a vice — to love myself, since I am a human being too.

—*Erich Fromm*

• • •

Happy is the man that findeth wisdom, and the man that getteth understanding. (Proverbs 3:13)

• • •

Caring about others, running the risk of feeling, and leaving and impact on people brings happiness.

—*Rabbi Harold Kushner*

• • •

Life is divided into three parts — that which was, which is, and which will be. Let us learn from the past to profit by the present, and from the present to live better for the future.

—*Wordsworth*

• • •

It is difficult to make a man miserable while he feels he is worthy of himself and claims kindred to the great God who made him.

—Abraham Lincoln

• • •

God asks no man whether he will accept life.
    That is not the choice.
    You must take it.
The only choice is how.

—Henry Ward Beecher

• • •

...we inhabit an invisible spiritual environment from which our help comes, our soul being mysteriously one with a larger one whose instruments we are.

—Henry James

• • •

This is what I found out about religion: it gives you courage to make the decisions you must make in a crisis and the confidence to leave the results to a higher Power. Only by trust in God can a man carrying responsibility find repose.

—Dwight D. Eisenhower

• • •

I hope I shall possess firmness and virtue enough to maintain what I consider the most enviable of all titles, the character of an honest man.

—George Washington

• • •

Public opinion is a weak tyrant compared with our own private opinion. What a man thinks of himself, that it is which indicates his fate.

—Thoreau

• • •

295

To be courageous requires no exceptional qualifications, no magic formula, no special combination of time, place and circumstance. It is an opportunity that sooner or later is presented to us all.

...each man must decide for himself the course he will follow. The stories of past courage can define that ingredient — they can teach, they can offer hope, they can provide inspiration. But they cannot supply courage itself. For this each man must look into his own soul.

—John F. Kennedy

• • •

Heaven is the vision of fulfilled desire,
Hell but the shadow of a soul on fire.

—Omar Khayyam

• • •

The thoughts of the Soul are not ideas, but creative powers... the more the Soul lives in the light of the spirit, "turned towards" that which is above itself, the more creative it becomes.

—Plotinus

• • •

The author of <u>Cloud of Unknowing</u> says:

"For all other creatures and their works, yea, and of the works of God's self, may a man through grace have a full head of knowing, and well he can think of them: but of God Himself can no man think. And therefore I would leave all that thing that I can think, and choose to my love that thing I cannot think. For why; He may well be loved, but not thought. By love may He be gotten and holden; but by thought never."

• • •

Religion, not in the conventional but in the broadest sense, helps me to have a glimpse of the divine essence. This glimpse is impossible without full development of the moral sense. Hence religion and morality are, for me, synonymous terms.

—*Mohandas K. Gandhi*

•••

The image of God is found essentially and personally in all mankind. Each possesses it whole, entire and undivided... we are the image of God... the source in us of all our life...

—*Jan van Ruysbroeck*

•••

No individual, however great, can be an exhaustive expression of God but each individual is a distinctive expression and brings out a characteristic of God's being. It may be said that every human being is unique and answers to a specific need in God.

—*Sarvepalli Radharkrishnan*

•••

Thou art thyself a fragment torn from God. Thou hast a portion of Him within thyself.

—*Epictetus*

•••

God wants only one thing in the whole world, the thing which it needs; ...that thing is to find the innermost part of the noble spirit of man clean and ready for Him to accomplish the divine purpose therein. He has all power in heaven and earth, but the power to do His work in man against man's will, He has not got.

—*John Tauler*

•••

Grant, O Father, to our minds, to climb to that august abode, grant us to visit the Fountain of Good, grant that finding the Light, we may open wide and fix on Thee the eyes of our souls. Scatter the mists and the heaviness of the earthly mass, and shine out with Thine own splendour; for Thou art the Serene, Thou art the tranquil resting place of the steadfast; to behold Thee is the aim. Thou art at once the beginning, the carrier, the guide, the pathway and the end.

—*Boethius*

• • •

AN INDIAN PRAYER
O Great Spirit:

Let me walk in beauty, and make my eyes ever behold the red and purple sunset.

Make my hands respect the things you have made and my ears sharp to hear your voice.

Make me wise so that I may understand the things you have taught my people.

Let me learn the lessons you have hidden in every leaf and rock.

I seek strength, not to be greater than my brother, but to fight my greatest enemy — myself.

Make me always ready to come to you with clean hands and straight eyes.

• • •

The creative force, which produces and sustain all that is, reveals itself to me in a way in which I do not get to know it elsewhere... as something which desires to be creative within me.

—Albert Schweitzer

•••

I have sworn upon the altar of God, eternal hostility against every form of tyranny over the mind of men.

—Thomas Jefferson

•••

Whatever is, is in God, and nothing can exist or be conceived without God.

—Spinoza

•••

... just as you mustn't try to heal the eyes without the head or the head without the body, so neither must you try to heal the body without the soul.

—Plato

•••

No man has a right to lead such a life of comtemplation as to forget in his own ease the service due to his neighbor; nor has any man a right to be so immersed in active life as to neglect the contemplation of God.

—St. Augustine

•••

299

Wherefore when you find yourself in this confidence with our Lord, stay there without moving yourself to make sensible acts, either of the understanding or of the will; for this simple love of confidence and the rest of the spirit... contains by excellence all that you go hither and thither to satisfy your taste. It is better to rest here than to watch elsewhere.

—*St. Francis de Sales*

● ● ●

Truly it is Life that shines forth in all things!
Vast, heavenly, unthinkable form, it shines forth...
It is farther than the far, yet near at hand,
Set down in the secret place of the heart...
Not by sight is it grasped, nor even by speech,
But by the peace of knowledge, one's nature purified—
In that way, by meditating, one does behold Him who is
without form.

—*The Upanishads*

Steven Hawking, noted scientist who is working on the Theory of Everything, said the theory would "...be the ultimate triumph of human reason, for then we would know the mind of God." Asked why man needs God and has continued to search for him for centuries, Hawking comments, "Everyone has some set of beliefs, some basis on which they act. We're limited in what we can do and are comparatively short-lived, and we have to believe in something outside ourselves. We may call this set of beliefs God, Marxism, Leninism or scientific rationalism, but that's largely a matter of words. They all serve the same need, of providing a framework with which to interpret the world we find ourselves in."

● ● ●

Peace—

When the collective intelligence of the human race arrives at a concept of freedom, the human race will be free, and not until then. There may be those who believe we can compel freedom, but we cannot do so. We would only find ourselves exchanging one kind of bondage for another.

—*Ernest Holmes*

• • •

Let every man pray that he may in some true sense be a solider of fortune; that he may have the good fortune to spend his energies and his life in the service of his fellow-men in order that he may die to be recorded upon the rolls of those who have not thought of those whom they served.

—*Woodrow Wilson*

• • •

When you are inspired by some great purpose, some extraordinary project, all your thoughts break their bonds; Your mind transcends limitations, your consciousness expands in every direction, and you find yourself in a new, great and wonderful world. Dormant forces, faculties and talents become alive, and you discover yourself to be a greater person by far than you ever dreamed yourself to be.

—**Patanjali**

• • •

Appendix

Appendix

The following is an abbreviated list of sources you may want to pursue:

- *Contemporary Religious Poetry*, (c) 1987, Paulist Press

- *Bartlett's Familiar Quotations*, Pocket Books, Inc.

- *What God Is Like*, (c) 1973 by James Dillet Freeman, a beautiful, hardcover, 115-page book of sensitive, spiritual verses. Published by Unity Books. Write for their catalog: Unity, Unity Village, Missouri, 64065. They also publish two montly periodicals: Daily Word and Unity Magazine, which include inspirational poetry by freelance poets.

- *The Prophet* by Kahlil Gibran, published by Alfred A. Knopf, is an invaluable masterpiece of philosophical poems. An addition to that work is the paperback collection, "The Treasury of Kahlil Gibran," published by Carol Publishing Group.

- *The Art of Creative Thinking*, by Wilferd A. Peterson, author of "The Art of Living," published by Hay House, (c) 1991. Contains his essays with heart-stirring messages.

•*Find and Use Your Inner Power*, by Emmet Fox, re-printed in paperback by Harper/S/F, is also a fountain of sagacity.

•*The Treasure Chest*, (c) 1965 by Charles L. Wallis is another inspirational book still in print by Harper and Row that lives up to its title.

•*The Harper Religious and Inspirational Quotation Companion*, (c) 1989, compiled by Margaret Pepper, published by Harper and Row, is a paragon of works by great thinkers.

•*Salesian Inspirational Books*, published every two months, contain a wealth of creative, mood-lifting poems by a variety of gifted poets. These booklets are especially helpful when you need an appropriate verse to refer to a holiday. For information, write Salesian Missions, 2 Lefevre Lane, New Rochelle, NY 10801.

•The Bible League publishes a series of booklets for a nominal fee that contain scripture truths and comforting statements in dealing with problems in life. An excellent booklet to have when preparing a memorial service is *God Understands: Scripture Truths for those in Sorrow*. Write or call for catalog, (708) 331-2094. 16801 Van Dam Road, South Holland, Ill. 60473. To order by phone: (800) 334-7017.

• *Ideals Magazine* features the works of many known and unknown poets. This magazine also is a valuable source for holiday material. Besides subscription, it can be found in many libraries. Ideals, PO Box 14800, Nashville, TN 37213-8000.

• *Emerson's Essays*, Harper/Collins

• *Science of Mind Magazine* does not feature poetry, but does contain stimulating affirmations. Science of Mind Magazine, PO Box 75127, Los Angeles, CA 90075.

HUMOR:
• *Reader's Digest*
• *Big Book of Jewish Humor* (c) 1965 Harper and Row
• *The Quotable Quote Book* (1990) Citadel Press

FOR ENVIRONMENTALIST GROUPS:
• Write to World Happiness and Cooperation, PO Box 1153, Anacortes, WA 98221 for a list of their books on this subject.

• The Presbyterian Church (USA) has an enterprising "Peacemaking Program" with copious brochures and material available. Write for their Peacemaking Resource List. Presbyterian Peacemaking Program, Social Justice and Peacemaking Ministry Unit, 100 Witherspoon St., Louisville, KY 40202-1396. (502) 569-5786.

Epilogue

This is a new age coming into expression, and perhaps the world is ready for a new system of cohesiveness in incorporating long-standing concepts and new philosophies into a union that neither shreds the old nor creates dogmatism in the new.

Because God, the creator of our universe, supplies us with no divinely measured allotment of love, we can generously embrace all within our circle of life with love radiations. And as love knows no bounds, we can extend the eternal fountain of unreserved love to all humanity, our brothers and sisters, fellow pilgrims on this small planet, Earth.

We need not withhold and limit the unlimited that God gives us freely, without a price. Let us learn to use this gift unconditionally through the practice of loving thoughts, actions and prayers for the welfare of all mankind.

—*Pat Warner*

A

Achievement, 167

Affirmation, 43, 52-53, 121, 123

Amen, 59

Amen substitution, 146

American flag. *See* Flag

American's Creed, The, 188

Appendix, 303

Arlington National Cemetery, 191

Armed Forces Day, 171, 173-174. *See also* Patriotic Holidays

Armistice Day. *See* Veterans Day

Awards, community service, 209-210

Axioms. *See* Maxims

B

Beecher, Henry Ward, 117, 182, 295

Belief in God, 290-292

Bell, Alexander Graham, 209, 232

Bellamy, Rev. Francis, 182

Benediction, 44, 145-156

Bible subjects, 243-271
    Abundance
    Achievement
    Belief
    Blessings
    Brotherhood
    Comfort
    Courage
    Divine Order
    Dominion
    Faith
    Fear
    Forgiveness
    Freedom
    Gifts
    Glory
    God's Presence
    Goodness
    Guidance
    Harmony
    Healing
    Health
    Illumination
    Instruction
    Joy
    Justice
    Light
    Love
    New Day
    Oneness
    Patience
    Peace
    Positive Attitude
    Praise
    Prayer
    Protection
    Rejoice
    Strength
    Success
    Trust
    Wisdom
    Words
    Works
    World Peace

Blake, William, 117

Blessings
    closing, 145-156
    table, 135-141

Boethius, 298

Bradford, Gov. William, 206

Bunyan, John, 38

Bush, Pauline, 122-123
Business meeting, 215

C

Candles, memorial services, 221-222
Cervantes, 284
Chaplain
    Army, 145
    composing tips, 49-59
    conventions, 159-165
    defined, 14-15, 25-26
    speaking tips, 63-65
    of United States, 30-31, 127, 129
    U.S. Senate, 128, 131
Church bulletin fillers, 275-286
Clarke, James Freeman, 7
Clergy
    composing tips, 49-59
    Honorarium, 17,19
    meetings, 18-19
    speaking tips, 63-65
Closing thoughts, 44, 275-286
Clow, Pauling S., 125-126
Clubs, non-sectarian, 32-36
Columbus, Christopher, 205-206
Columbus, Ferdinand, 205-206
Columbus Day, 205-206. *See also Special events*
Commemorations, 222-223
Commemorative days, 192-208
Committee recognition, 165-169
Composing tips, 49-59
Conflict, 214
Confucius, 291
Congress, 29
Congressional Research Report Service for Congress, 31

Convention
    club chaplain, 159-162
    committee recognition, 165-169
    invocation, 163
    member/delegate recognition, 164
    memorials, 223-225
Convention, *See also* Invocation
Coolidge, Calvin, 285
Coping, 239
Creative power, 53-54, 153, 299
Creed, The American's, 188
Cultural diversity, 33-36, 195-196
Cushing, Cardinal Richard, 131

D

Death, *See* Memorial services
Delegate recognition, 164-165
Delivery, 62-65
De Molinos, Miguel, 123
De Sales, St. Frances, 39, 152, 300
Desiderata, 112
Devotional, 43-47
Drummond, Henry, 92, 153
Dubina, Michael, 118-119
Duffy, Nona Keen, 172, 184, 187
Durant, Will, 294

E

Eisenhower, Dwight D., Pres., 173, 182, 191, 295
Election invocation, 213
Emerson, Ralph Waldo, 277, 280, 291
Environmentalist groups, 217

Epictetus, 85, 297
Epistle of Paul, 289-290
E. Pluribus Unum, 34, 36
Eulogy. *See* Memorial services

F
Fillmore, Charles, 292
First Amendment, 30-31
Flag, 170
Flag Act, 180-181
Flag Day, 171, 178-185. *See also*
    Patriotic holidays
Flag definitions, 181
Ford, Henry, 277
Ford, Rev. James David, 127
Fosdick, Harry Emerson, 38, 120
Fox, Emmet, 116
Franklin, Benjamin, 30, 36, 189,
    277
Freeman, James Dillet, 235, 290
Fromm, Erich, 294
Fuller, 285
Funeral. *See* Memorial services

G
Gandhi, Mahatma, 39, 84, 297
Gelasius, Pope, 196
Gibran, Kahil, 39, 222, 229, 231
Gilson, Roy Rolfe, 117
Glascow, Arnold, 276, 283
Goldsmith, Oliver, 277
Grace, (Table blessings)
    brief, 138, 141
    chef compliment, 161
    defined, 44, 135
    with scriptures, 136-141
Guest, Edgar A., 208

Guthman, Rabbi, Dr. Sidney S.,
    36, 89, 190

H
Halverson, Rev. Richard C., 128
Hancock, John, 186
Hargesheimer, Rev. Tom, 129
Harrison, Benjamin, 205
Hawking, Steven, 300
Heitman, Willamae M., 233
Heschel, Abraham Joshua, 39
Holidays
    defined, 171
    Independence Day, 171,
        186-190
    Labor Day, 204
    Lincoln's Birthday, 198-199
    Martin Luther King, Jr. Day,
        195
    Memorial Day, 174-178
    New Year's Day, 192-194
    patriotic, 171-191
    Thanksgiving Day, 206-208
    Veterans Day, 171, 191
    Washington's Birthday,
        199-210. *See also* Special
        events
Holmes, Ernest, 301
Holms, Oliver Wendell, 283, 294
Holy Bible. See Bible
Homily preparation, 51-53
Honorarium, 17, 19
Howe, E.W., 276
Hugo, Victor, 39

I
Independence Day, 171, 186-
    190. *See also* Patriotic
    holidays

Indian prayer, 298
Indian Proverb, 149
Individualized prayers, 121-131
Inspiration, 45, 105-120
Invocation
    convention, 163
    dedicated service, 167, 212
    defined, 45-47
    Flag Day, 185
    general, 89-104
    Independence Day, 190
    internal conflict, 214
    introduction, 57-60, 71-75
    New Year, 194
    newly elected officers, 166,
      211
    opening meetings, 77-104
    sales meetings, 216
    specialized groups, 209-217
    writing ideas, 51-59
Izzard, Wes, 277

J
James, Henry, 295
James, William, 83
Jefferson, Thomas, 29, 186, 299
Jesus, 292
Jewish War Veterans, 127, 175
Julian of Norwich, 39, 149

K
Kennedy, John F., 202, 296
Khayyam, Omar, 296
King, Dr. Martin Luther Jr., 195
Kushner, Rabbi Harold, 294

L
Labor Day, 204. *See also*
    Holidays

Law Day, 202-203. *See also*
    Special Events
Liberty Bell, 186
Liebman, Joshua Loth, 239
Lincoln, Abraham, 207, 295
Lincoln's Birthday, 198-199
Logan, John A., 175-177
Longfellow, Henry Wadsworth,
    152-153
Lord's Prayer, The, 238
Love, 116, 261, 293
Lozano, Mimi, 114-115

M
Macauley, 282
Madison, President, 206-207
Marshall, General George C., 29
Marshall, Peter, 130-131
Maxims, 275-286
Meditation, 46, 123-126
Meetings,
    business, 215
    chaplain, 14-15
    new officers, 166
    opening, 13-14, 71-131
    outside clergy, 18-19
    presiding officer, 13-14
    sales, 216
    special events, 16-17
Member achievement, 167-169
Member recognition, 164
Memorial Day, 171, 174-178. *See
    also* Patriotic holidays
Memorial services, 221-239
Miller, Joaquin, 206
Molinos, Miguel de, 123
Morley, Christopher, 281

Moses, 292
Muller, Chancellor Robert, 217
N
Names of God, 32-33
National colors, 181
National ensign, 181
National flag, 181. *See also* Flag
National motto, 30, 34, 36
National standard, 181
New Day, 261-262, 293
New Genesis, 217
Newman, Cardinal, 277
New Year's Day, 192-194
New Year's resolutions, 193
Noble, C., 281
Non-sectarian persuasion, 32-36

O
Officer
    presiding, 13-14, 29
Old Glory, 172
Old Saint Paul's Church, 112
Opening Ceremonies, 13-15
Opening meeting
    inspirations, 105-120
    introductions, 71-75
    invocations, 77-104
Organizations
    environmentalists, 217
    memorial services, 233-234
    service awards, 209-210
    United Nations, 217
    See also Resources, 305

P
Page, William Tyler, 188
Pascal, B., 276
Patanjali, 301

Patriotic holidays, 171-191
Paul the Apostle, 279
Paulson, J. Sig. 226
Peace, 301
Personal recognition, 210
Plato, 153, 299
Pledge of Allegiance, 170
Pledge Law, 173
Plotinus, 43, 296
Poetry and Prose
    Angel of Patience, The, 230
    Candle in the Night, A., 236
    Change, 237
    Commonness of Love and Lure, 118-119
    Count Blessings, 109
    Day Worthwhile, A, 106
    Desiderata, 112
    Do Not Judge Too Hard, 111
    Eternal Vision, 226
    Everlasting Light, The, 227
    Flag Speaks, The, 184
    Food for Thought, 231
    Forefather's Day, 208
    Guidepaths to Peace, 119
    I Love America, 172
    Indian Prayer, An, 298
    Life is Everlasting, 231
    Life's Splendor, 108
    Love, 116
    Madam President, 20-21
    Make a Pearl, 120
    memorial (untitled), 228
    My Country, 189
    Our Flag, 178
    Perception, 114
    Power of Littles, The, 110
    Prayer of St. Francis of Assisi, A, 228

Slow me down, Lord, 116
Time is, 115
Traveller, The, 235
We The People, 187
What God is Like, 290
What is Life?, 229
Winding Way, The, 107
Prayer
    Bible text, 243-271
    by notables, 127-131
    defined, 46-47
    delivery, 55-59, 63-65
    individualized, 121-131
    introductions to, 51-54
    for meetings, 69-73, 215-217
    public schools, 29-31
    quotations on, 38-40
    Supreme Court ruling, 29-31
    writing tips, 49-59
Prayer protocol
    cultural diversity, 33-36
    names of God, 32-33
    prayer, 29-40
    reasons to pray, 37-40
Preparation, homily, 51-57
Presiding officer, meetings,
    13-14
Prophet, The, 229
Protection, 156, 266
Province Bell. *See* Liberty Bell
Public schools prayer, 31

R
Radharkrishnan, Sarvepalli, 297
Rafferty. Dr. Max, 31
Rayburn, S., 282
Reasons to pray, 37-40

Recognition, personal, 210
Resolutions, New Years, 192-193
Riley, James Whitcomb, 228
Roosevelt, Theodore, 198, 292
Russell, Bertrand, 26

S
Saadi, 276
St. Augustine, 113, 152, 197, 299
St. Francis of Assisi prayer, 228
St. Francis de Sales, 39, 152, 300
St. Patrick's Day, 201-202. *See
    also* Special events
St. Teresa of Avila, 39
Salesian Missions, 239
Sanskrit, 293
Sarnoff, David, 279
Schuck, John J., 237
Schweitzer, Albert, 153, 299
Science, 231
Scott, Walter, 193
Scripture verses, 243-271
Seneca, 282
Service awards, 209-210
Service organizations, 212
Shakespeare, William, 294
Shaw, George Bernard, 83, 154
Sochatt, 285
Socrates, 38
Sparks, 282
Speaking, success tips, 63-65
Special events
    Armed Forces Day, 171,
        173-174
    Columbus Day, 205-206
    commemorative days, 192
    Community Service
        Awards, 209-210

conventions, 159
election invocation, 213
environmentalists, 217
Flag Day, 171, 179, 185
holidays, 171-208
Labor Day, 204
Law Day, 202-203
memorial services, 221-239
Presidents' Day, 192,
    198-201
St. Patrick's Day, 201-202
Valentine's Day, 196-198
Specialized groups, invocation,
    209-217
Spinoza, 299
Staff, Commander Caroline, 127,
    175
Stevenson, Robert Louis, 282
Supreme Court ruling, 29-31

T
Table blessing, *See* Grace
Taft, President, 180
Talbot, Leona, 178
Tauler, John, 297
Thanksgiving Day, 206-208
Thoreau, 154, 295
Tolstoy, Leo, 26, 291
Tomlinson, 283
Toynbee, Arnold J., 38
Truman, Harry S., 173
Twenty-third Psalm, The, 239

U
University for Peace
    (Costa Rica), 217
Unknown Soldier, 191

Upanishads, The, 300
U.S. Congress, 31
U.S. Constitution, 30-31

V
Valentine's Day, 196-198
Van Buren, Martin, 286
Van Dyke, Henry, 119, 152
Van Ruysbroeck, Jan, 297
Veterans Day, 171, 191. *See also*
    Patriotic holidays
Veteran's Medical Facility, 36
Vogel, Rev. George, 36
Von Braun, Dr. Wernher, 231

W
Ward, Barbara, 119
Washington, Booker T., 281
Washington, George, 28, 35, 37,
    186, 199-200, 295
Watts, Alan, 124
Whittier, John G. 230
Wilcox, Ella Wheeler, 120
Wilson, Woodrow, 180, 191, 301
Wine, Mary Stoner, 236
Wordsworth, 152, 294
World Happiness and
    Cooperation, 217
World peace, 270, 271, 291
Writing tips, 49-59, 275-286

GOOD GRACES

INVOCATIONS, INSPIRATIONS
and REFLECTIONS
for
Club Chaplains and Speakers

Order your copy now.

OTHOREAL PUBLISHING CO.
P.O. Box 2778
Seal Beach, CA 90740-1778

Please send_____ copies of *Good Graces* to:
Name:_____
Organization:_____
Title:_____
Address:_____
City:_____ State:____Zip:_____
Enclose check or money order for $16.95 for each book, plus $2 shipping for the first book, $1.50 for each additional book. Please add 7.75% sales tax to orders shipped to California addresses.
Satisfaction is fully guaranteed.
Canada: $18.95 plus shipping